FAMILIA

ULSTER GENEALOGICAL REVIEW

Ulster
Genealogical
& Historical
Guild

NUMBER 20
2004
THE MEMBERSHIP ASSOCIATION OF
ULSTER HISTORICAL FOUNDATION

FRONT COVER

Joy's Paper mill overlooking Belfast, 1806
Courtesy of the Trustees of the National Museums and Galleries of Northern Ireland.

Published 2004
by Ulster Historical Foundation
12 College Square East, Belfast, BT1 6DD
www.ancestryireland.com
www.booksireland.org.uk

ISBN 1 903688 52 3

Printed by ColourBooks Ltd
Design and production, Dunbar Design

CONTENTS

EDITORIAL

This issue of *Familia* is the twentieth that has been published since the first issue in 1985, a significant milestone. The original aim was to provide a forum in which family and local historians could not only read and learn about research on topics and publications in which they had a mutual interest but it would also serve as a facility for the publication of research they themselves undertook. This modestly ambitious aim has by and large been successful so, on the premise that 'if it ain't broke …' the format of this year's edition is very much along tried-and-tested lines. Eull Dunlop's review says as much.

The theme of ethnicity is a thread running through William Roulston and Pamela McIlveen's consideration of the original Jewish settlement in Belfast at the end of the nineteenth century and Michael Montgomery's discussion of how the original settlers from Ulster in eighteenth-century America have been identified by the terms applied to them. Alison Muir's detailed research on the manufacture of paper, and the uses of locally-manufactured paper, is a truly original piece of work on an aspect of the eighteenth century economy that was the background against which the forces of emigration are being increasingly seen. Paddy Fitzgerald's account of post-graduate teaching and learning on the theme of emigration is a reflection of how far the topic of emigration has come. William Roulston's re-creation of an eighteenth-century family, using the evidence available, provides a more-than-useful model for others to follow.

This growth has been due in no small measure to the research and published writings over the last twenty years of Kerby A. Miller. It is entirely fitting, therefore, that Professor Miller should review the new volume of essays on the theme of assisted emigration edited by Paddy Duffy who, with his co-editor Gerald Moran, whose most recent publication is also reviewed, has brought deserving attention to the area of assisted emigration from Ireland. Brenda Collins' review of

Frank McCorry's published researches on church registers in Co. Armagh will have a broad interest, as will Fred Rankin's report on a new work on Quaker churches throughout Ireland. The other reviews reflect the broad canvas of historical topics that continue to feature in the journal and which interest and are of use to our readership.

TREVOR PARKHILL
KEEPER OF HISTORY
ULSTER MUSEUM

NOTES ON CONTRIBUTORS

BRENDA COLLINS is Research Officer at the Irish Linen Centre, Lisburn Museum.

EULL DUNLOP is a former teacher involved in local history in mid-Antrim and beyond.

PATRICK FITZGERALD is Lecturer & Development Officer at the Centre for Migration Studies, Ulster American Folk Park, Omagh.

PAMELA McILVEEN is a QUB graduate who has recently been researching aspects of Jewish history in Northern Ireland.

KERBY A. MILLER is Professor of History at the University of Missouri, Columbia.

MICHAEL MONTGOMERY is Emeritus Professor of English, University of South Carolina.

ALISON MUIR is Paper Conservator in the Ulster Museum currently researching a doctoral thesis at The Queen's University of Belfast.

J. FRED RANKIN, a retired businessman, serves on the Ulster Historical Foundation Publications Committee and has published extensively on local and ecclesiastical history.

WILLIAM ROULSTON is Research Officer, Ulster Historical Foundation.

TREVOR PARKHILL is Keeper of History, Ulster Museum, Belfast.

RABBI JACOB SHACHTER 1886–1971

Jacob Shachter was Rabbi and Spiritual Head of the Jewish Community in Belfast and Northern Ireland 1926–53. This portrait, by R. Taylor Carson, was commissioned by the Belfast Hebrew Congregation on the 25th anniversary of his ministry. It was presented to the Ulster Museum in 2002 by his son, Israel Shachter.

COURTESY OF THE TRUSTEES OF THE NATIONAL MUSEUMS AND GALLERIES OF NORTHERN IRELAND

Researching Belfast Jewish Families
c. 1850–*c.* 1930

PAMELA McILVEEN AND WILLIAM ROULSTON

THIS BELFAST JEWISH COMMUNITY is currently celebrating the centenary of the opening of the synagogue in Annesley Street, just off Carlisle Circus in the north of the city. Opened in August 1904 by Sir Otto Jaffe, for many Russian and Polish immigrants the synagogue proved to be something of a refuge after a hard day's work in what were often demanding circumstances. Journalist Martin Sieff, a former *Belfast Telegraph* reporter now with United Press International, sums up the hold of the synagogue for him and for many members of the Jewish congregation in the city:

> *To me it really was a shul from the long centuries of Galut [exile] with all the romance, atmosphere, and mystery that accrued.*[1]

It may therefore be timely to remember that there was a quite substantial settlement of Jewish people who arrived and resided, largely in north Belfast, in the last quarter of the nineteenth and first few decades of the twentieth centuries. In this context, it may be appropriate to consider the question of how a researcher might set about reconstructing Jewish families in Northern Ireland in the late nineteenth and early twentieth centuries. It is important to emphasise that the approach adopted is very much that of the genealogist. At the same time it is not our intention to give a detailed presentation of all the sources that could be used to research Jewish ancestors in Northern Ireland, but rather to give some pointers as to how the history of Jewish families in the province might be explored further. Genealogical sources are of course about people so this perspective should be of interest to social historians as well as those researching specific Jewish families. The geographical focus will be on Belfast because this is where the great majority of Jewish families in the northern part of Ireland lived.

HISTORICAL BACKGROUND

The Jewish community in Belfast differed immensely in size and chronology from its counterparts in Dublin and Great Britain. Whilst England can date the arrival of Jews to the medieval period, the earliest record of a Jewish resident in what is now Northern Ireland is the solitary figure of a tailor – Manuel Lightfoot – living in Belfast in 1652.[2] There are virtually no records of any other Jews in Belfast until the middle of the nineteenth century. The earliest Belfast entry in a register of Jewish births kept in Dublin is that of Meir Levy, to whom a male child was born in 1849. In the *Belfast and Province of Ulster Directory* of 1852 Meir Levy & Co., drapers and hatters, were listed at 61 High Street. The Jewish population in Belfast remained small, however: in 1861 it was only 11, while in 1881 it was still only 61. It was also mainly German in origin.

The immigration of German Jews into Ulster predates the larger eastern European immigration by about twenty to thirty years. Daniel Joseph Jaffe, a Hamburg merchant, came to Belfast in 1845 with the intention of establishing contacts for the purchase of linen goods.[3] By 1852 the Jaffe family had moved to Belfast and opened a linen house in the city, shipping linen back to the family offices in Dundee, Paris, Hamburg, Leipzig and New York and agents further afield in Russia and South America.[4] In the aforementioned *Belfast and Province of Ulster Directory* of 1852 Jaffa [sic] Brothers, merchants, are listed at 4 Fountain Lane in the city

Although small in number and present for just over half a century, the German Jews who came to Belfast from the 1850s to the 1870s were the foundation of a permanent Jewish community in Northern Ireland. They provided lay-leadership and tangible financial and charitable support to their eastern European co-religionists. Following the

May Laws introduced in Russia in 1882, hundreds of thousands of Jews fled westwards. Some 150,000 eastern European Jews arrived in Britain in less than 25 years, several hundred of whom made their way to the north of Ireland, mainly to Belfast. In 1901 there were 708 Jews in Belfast and by 1911 the number had risen to 1,139, nearly all of whom were Ashkenazi Jews from central and eastern Europe. Many of these Jews worked in a concentrated number of trades as tailors, shoemakers and cabinetmakers and a large number were travelling salesmen. When the first census was held in Northern Ireland in 1926 there were 1,149 Jews in Belfast.

THE JAFFE FAMILY

When studying Jewish families in Belfast it is difficult not to devote a disproportionate amount of time to one family in particular. The wealth of sources available to anyone wishing to research the Jaffe family tree is remarkable. The family claimed descent from a Medieval religious scholar, Rabbi Mordechai Jaffe of Prague, and through him from the greatest of all Jewish Bible scholars, the eleventh-century Rashi.[5] Perhaps the most famous, they were also the first German Jewish linen merchants to settle and trade in the city, and certainly the most successful. Studying the Jaffe family opens avenues into records of Jewish participation in trade, industry, commerce, politics, charity work, education, local government and the arts. Both Louis Hyman and Bernard Shillman give accounts of the family's beginnings in and departure from Ireland.[6] The Jewish quarter of the City Cemetery is the final resting place of the founder and organiser of the city's Jewish congregation – Daniel Joseph Jaffe, born in Mecklenburg, Schwerin, on 19 August 1809. Daniel Joseph's son Martin held the first Jewish services in Northern Ireland in his Holywood home under the auspices of the British Chief Rabbi, but it was his father who, on 7 July 1871, laid the foundation stone of the synagogue in Great Victoria Street. Daniel Joseph Jaffe died in Nice on 21 January 1874 but was buried in Belfast thanks to his son Martin's success in securing the plot of land in City Cemetery which was to become the Jewish Cemetery.

In many ways, however, it is the legacy of Daniel Joseph's son – Otto

– that often overshadows his father's testimony. Otto was described most famously by his contemporaries as 'shrewd, sharp-witted, far seeing and [whilst] almost parsimonious in business, he is lavish in unostentatious charities'.[7] He was elected a city councillor in 1894, was elected as Belfast's first Lord Mayor in 1899 (the first incumbent of the title under the new status of the city as a county borough). He was knighted after his first term, served as High Sheriff and was re-elected as Lord Mayor in 1904. Sir Otto had a deep interest in education. The Jaffe school, by his stipulation, was not exclusively Jewish – Catholics and Protestants attended as pupils and served as staff and on the management board. He was also a pioneer in the foundation of Belfast's Technical College and contributed £4,000 to Queen's University.

Otto Jaffe made a huge contribution to the consolidation of the Jewish community in the province. As life president of the Belfast Congregation he contributed the majority of the funds required to build a new synagogue to house the two separate Great Victoria Street and Regent Street congregations. On 31 August 1904 Sir Otto opened the new synagogue in Annesley Street, Carlisle Circus. As JP, member of the Harbour Board, member of the first senate of Queen's University, Governor of the Royal Victoria Hospital, German Consul in Belfast, twice Lord Mayor and knighted, Sir Otto Jaffe was the representation of Jewish civic virtue; a fully integrated philanthropist, leader of both his co-religionists and non-Jewish citizens. Yet Otto Jaffe has no headstone in Northern Ireland. In 1916, after 25 years of service in the Belfast Corporation, he moved to England following intimidation aimed at the family during the First World War because of their German roots.[8] The family's loyalty was without question: they returned to support the war effort in the mainland with Otto's son Arthur Daniel serving in the British army. Sir Otto died and was cremated in London in 1929.

CIVIL REGISTRATION

The main sources of basic family history information about the Jewish community in Belfast and Northern Ireland in this period are the civil registers of births, deaths and marriages. All births, deaths and marriages were registered from 1864. Non-Catholic marriages are registered from 1 April 1845. Not only did this mean Protestant marriages, it also included marriages conducted in the newly-created registry offices. Here we find the first marriage in Belfast involving members of the Jewish community. This was the marriage on 15 November 1859 of Marcus Robert Mendlessohn and Malvina Jaffe. Mendlessohn was a merchant whose address was given as Donegall Square East. His father was Robert Mendlesson, also a merchant, a fairly general term for anyone involved in business. Malvina, whose residence was given as Holywood, was the daughter of Daniel Joseph Jaffe.

In 1875, four years after the opening of the Great Victoria Street synagogue in Belfast, the first recorded marriage conducted under its auspices took place: that of George Betzold of Wilmont Terrace, a linen merchant, and Anne Rosenbaum of Ulsterville Avenue. Around 150 Jewish marriages took place in Belfast in the period between 1875 and 1921.[9] Nearly all of them were conducted under the auspices of the Great Victoria Street and Annesley Street synagogues. Only two marriages – in 1902 and 1903 – are recorded for the short-lived Regent Street synagogue.

Birth registers for Northern Ireland are available from 1864 in the General Register Office in Chichester Street in Belfast. An official birth certificate will not indicate the religion of the child. It is therefore not possible to search specifically for the births of Jewish children. The Ulster Historical Foundation has a relatively small number of civil births on its database, but, during research, the following was discovered which is of some interest. This is the birth record of Chaim (or Chayim as it was written in the certificate) Herzog, son of Isaac Herzog, the Jewish rabbi, and Sarah Hillman – born on 17 September 1918 at 2 Norman Villas, Cliftonpark Avenue in north Belfast. Chaim Herzog of course became president of Israel in 1983; he died in 1997.

Death registers for Northern Ireland are also available in the General Register Office in Belfast from 1864. Irish death certificates are fairly uninformative: the name, age, marital status and occupation of the deceased, the date, place and cause of death, and the name and qualification of the informant are provided. The indexes to civil death registers usefully provide the age of the deceased.

CENSUS RECORDS

Beginning in 1821, a census was held in Ireland every ten years until 1911. However, the earliest complete census surviving for the whole of Ireland is from no earlier than 1901. Censuses for the thirty-year period 1821–51 were almost entirely destroyed in Dublin when the Public Record Office was burned in the Four Courts fire in June 1922, while those for 1861–91 were pulped on government orders during the First World War. The originals of both the 1901 and 1911 censuses are available in the National Archives in Dublin. At present only the 1901 census on microfilm is available in the Public Record Office in Belfast. The 1926 census for Northern Ireland was also intentionally destroyed.

To take as an example of the nature of the information contained in census records 13 Hopefield Avenue in north Belfast in 1911 may be used. The head of the household was Frank Wine and he lived there with his wife Julia and their children, Bertram and Sybil. There were three other occupants of the house. Mark Sugden a visiting wallpaper merchant, and two servants, Margaret Crawford and Eliza Drennan. Particularly useful about census returns is that they give the place of birth. For those born outside the British Isles this will be no more specific than the country. Thus we see that Frank Wine was born in Russia, not necessarily the Russia we understand today due to changes in political boundaries. His wife, however, was born in Manchester and we can possibly surmise that Frank stopped off there for some time prior to coming to Ireland. It is interesting to note that Mark Sugden was also born in Manchester.

By cross-referencing the information in this census return to civil birth registers we find that Bertram Wine was born on 10 March 1908 at 44 Orient Gardens, while Sybil was born on 31 October 1910 at Hopefield Avenue (both in Belfast). These registers also provide us with Julia's maiden name, Nathan. At least one other child was born: Beatrice Flora on 16 June 1913 when the family was living at 11 Easton Crescent. Three children born at three different addresses in the space of five years is an illustration of the housing mobility of the population in Belfast at this time, a phenomenon not just confined to the Jewish community.

SCHOOL RECORDS

School records provide a fascinating insight into the education of Jewish children in Belfast. The registers of Regent Street School, afterwards known as the Jaffe School, date from 1898, with the first pupils beginning classes on 10 March of that year. Both male and female registers are available for inspection in the Public Record Office of Northern Ireland, from 1898 to the 1940s for boys and the 1950s for girls.[10] The information contained in the registers includes the name, address, religion and date of birth of the pupil, the occupation, but unfortunately not the name of the father, and the date of entrance to the school. The name of the former school attended, if applicable, is also stated. There is also a useful column entitled, 'Destination of pupil'. In many cases this was entered simply as 'another school', 'gone to work', 'technical college' or 'apprenticeship'. However, a significant number of pupils emigrated. In many cases it will simply say, 'emigrated'. Occasionally more specific information will be provided. For example, the sisters, Fanny and Edith Appleton of Perth Street, who started school on 10 April 1907, emigrated to South Africa. Maurice Tyterbaum of Hillman Street, who started school on 23 September 1912 emigrated to America.

The school was not exclusively Jewish. An examination of the first boys' register, covering the period 1898-1916, reveals that of the 500 pupils recorded 79, or approximately 16 per cent, were not from Jewish backgrounds. These were made up of 29 Presbyterians, 26 Roman Catholics, 20 Anglicans, three styled 'Christian' and one styled 'Protestant'. The Jaffe School was not the only elementary school attended by Jewish children. Indeed many of the elementary schools in north Belfast had Jewish pupils at one time or another. For secondary level education Jewish children attended schools such as Belfast Royal Academy and Royal Belfast Academical Institution.[11]

GRAVESTONE INSCRIPTIONS

Gravestone inscriptions are an immensely important source for studying family history. The earliest known gravestone to a Jew in Northern Ireland can be found in the graveyard attached to Derriaghy Church of

Ireland church. It commemorates the death of Nathaniel Kronheim on 18 September 1852 at the age of 80. The informative inscription reads:

Underneath lie the mortal remains of Nathaniel Kronheim Born in Prussia Silesia and an Israelite according to the flesh but converted by the grace of God to the faith of the gospel which he afterwards lived to promote in public and in private for the space of 20 years during 18 of which he was employed in Ireland and especially in Ulster as agent to The Society for Promoting Christianity Among the Jews. Thus did he endeavour to serve that Saviour in whom he believed and whom he loved until in death he could say 'Lord now lettest thou thy servant Depart in Peace according to thy word For mine eyes have seen thy salvation.' This monument has been erected by a few of his personal friends as a small memorial of affectionate regard. He departed to his rest on the 18th Sept. 1852 aged nearly 80 years.

There is also an inscription in Hebrew on the face of the column. It reads in translation: 'Pray for the peace of Jerusalem'.

Mention has already been made of the Jewish quarter of Belfast City Cemetery. The City Cemetery was opened on 1 August 1869 to provide burial space in a rapidly expanding industrial city where the longer established graveyards were becoming overcrowded. In the autumn of 1870 formal proposals were made regarding the walling-off of a section for burials of members of the Jewish community.[12] Martin Jaffe, Honorary Secretary of the Hebrew Congregation, was the principal representative of the Jewish community at the meetings involving the corporation. Final approval came in 1871. The names and addresses of those who purchased graves can still be accessed in the records at the City Cemetery office, and these are a useful indication of the geographical spread of many of the first Jewish immigrants.

Also of some interest and value is a set of gravestone recordings taken by John and Patrick Holden as far back as Sunday, 11 October 1955. Over 100 names are listed, together with dates of birth, if given, and dates of death. Occasionally some additional information is provided. It is noted, for example, that Daniel Joseph Jaffe was born at Schwerin and died at Nice. A copy of these inscriptions can be consulted in the Public Record Office of Northern Ireland.[13] The value of the names transcribed lies in the fact that vandalism has resulted in the destruction of many headstones in the Jewish section of Belfast City Cemetery, while others have apparently been removed.[14] This photograph was taken last summer and provides an indication of the damage that has been done.

The Jewish quarter at Belfast City Cemetery showing vandalised headstones.

The expansion of the Jewish population in Belfast by the early twentieth century created a need for a second cemetery. With a large proportion of the Jewish community living in the north of the city, consideration was given to acquiring a plot of land for a burial ground in this area. In 1909 an application for a cemetery in the Rural District of Carnmoney was made to Belfast Rural District Council.[15] Despite a letter of objection from the Reverend R. J. Clarke, rector of the parish of Carnmoney, who believed that there were already too many cemeteries in the area, the application was granted. Soon afterwards a site in Carnmoney was purchased by Samuel Freeman, a house furnisher from York Street, and Maurice Goldring, a financier in Donegall Street. Trustees were then appointed who, in addition to Freeman and Goldring, included Sir Otto Jaffe, Luis Berwitz, another house furnisher in York Street, and David Levinson of Clones, County Monaghan, a merchant. Following the opening of this second cemetery the Jewish quarter at Belfast City Cemetery was less frequently used. The graveyard at Carnmoney, protected by a high wall and a secure gate, is in very good condition.

Two headstones at Carnmoney with interesting inscriptions read: 'Deborah Fox, Founder and President of the Hebrew Benevolent Society' and 'Herman Fox, Honorary President of the Belfast Hebrew Congregation and President of the Belfast Board of Guardians'. They died on the 22 September 1923 and 10 August 1932 respectively.

Herman Fox, along with his wife Deborah, helped to organise the Belfast Hebrew Benevolent Society and the Belfast Hebrew Board of Guardians. These organisations are incredibly elusive to those searching for any written record of their purpose and activities. Yet among those members of the Jewish community who witnessed their work, their legacy is resolute. Members of the financially secure German Jewish families organised a support network (independent of the state Poor Law Guardians) which provided interest free loans or small gifts to Jewish families in financial need, many of whom were eastern European immigrants, to enable them to 'find their feet' and establish small businesses in their trades. Along with seasonal gifts from the Passover Relief Fund etc., and Hebrew Friendly Societies an intricate support network was established within the Jewish community which linked Jewish 'working class' tradesmen to the wealthier commercial German Jewish families. In Jewish society the synagogue formed the pivot around which a multitude of family run support groups worked to keep the heads of immigrant Jews above water in times of crisis. The experiences of individual members of the Jewish community were far from uniform, yet the collective experience of emigration and common religious belief gave the community a distinctive coherence by the beginning of the twentieth century.

The inscriptions of a number of headstones highlight two further areas of Jewish history in Northern Ireland which require much more intensive research, the current resources for which are admittedly quite sparse. These are the experiences of the community during the First and Second World Wars and the history of the Gibraltar Jews in Northern Ireland. Carnmoney cemetery holds the headstones of Flight Sergeant B.E. Samuels of the Royal Canadian Air Force, Albert Goldstone, 'lost in Action, Hamburg 1942', pilot Louis Sergai (who served in the American Forces) and the grave of Harris Sergai whose son Bennett Sergai was lost in action in the Great War (Harris's will makes mention of monies made payable to him by the American Government for the loss of his son). These headstones are in part testimony to Jewish loyalty towards the British war effort. We know that 50,000 Jews served in the British forces in World War One and that of this 1,596 were decorated.[16] Also, because of the propensity for a large number of Jews to work in civilian occupations and trades, a large majority were conscripted into service in England, thus the proportion of Jews in the armed forces in England was greater than in the general population.

The Gibraltarian Jews buried in Carnmoney include Isaac Rafael Attias, Joseph Benselum, Reuben Benggio and Leah Pariente. Jews had lived in Gibraltar in the fourteenth century. However, when the island passed to English control in 1713 the Jewish residents were expelled until 1749. At its height, in the middle of the nineteenth century, the Jewish community in Gibralter numbered 2,000, at a time when the colony's strategic importance was most acute. During the Second World War the Jewish community was evacuated with the rest of the inhabitants to other British territories. A very small number made their way to Northern Ireland, with Joseph Benselum even residing in Saintfield. There has however been little research into the numbers of Gibraltarian Jews that came to Northern Ireland (gravestones are admittedly only an indication of those who stayed).

WILLS AND TESTAMENTARY PAPERS

Prior to 1858 the administration of wills was the responsibility of the Church of Ireland. However, from 1858 the state assumed responsibility for this. Virtually all original wills 1858–1900 were destroyed in Dublin in 1922, but transcripts of wills probated at the district registries of Armagh, Belfast and Londonderry are available on microfilm in the Public Record Office of Northern Ireland. Genealogists use wills primarily to establish family links, but information contained in a will can extend far beyond this to give us an idea of the social, economic, religious and philanthropic activities of the testator. They also provide us with some idea of the wealth of Jewish families in Belfast at this time.

Daniel Joseph Jaffe died at Nice on 21 January 1874. On 9 February his will was proved at Belfast with his executors including Martin Jaffe and Joseph John Jaffe of Belfast, Otto Moses Jaffe of New York and Siegmund Armin Oppe of London. His effects in the United Kingdom were valued at the staggeringly high figure of £140,000. The wealth of the Jaffes should not give the impression that all Jewish families in Belfast were of similar means. In fact most Jews did not leave a will, leaving us with no information on their financial standing.

One who did make a will was Caroline Boas (wife of the German Jewish merchant Herman) who lived at Windsor Park. She died in 1916 and was buried at Carnmoney. Her will provides us an intricate picture of domestic Jewish life in Belfast in the second decade of the twentieth century. Her home life was no doubt similar to many 'middle class' Jewish homes in Northern Ireland throughout the first half of the last century, filled with the objects of suburban domesticity: family portraits, sterling silver teapots, a Sheffield candelabra and hand painted china. We can see from the wills and testaments of Herman Fox, Albert Cohen, Sophia Cohen and a multitude of others that charitable organisations were supported by individual gifts bequeathed in wills or donated seasonally, like the Passover Relief Fund. The wills of Daniel Joseph Jaffe, the Cohens, Herman Fox, Harris Sergie and Samuel Freeman include generous bequests to local hospitals.

HOME AFFAIRS FILES

The papers generated by the Ministry of Homes Affairs in the new Northern Ireland government, created in 1921, form a vast and, as far as genealogists are concerned, under-used source. Part of the reason for this is the lack of a comprehensive index to all of the files. It was not possible in the course of research for this article to examine the early documents systematically, but just glancing through the PRONI list a number of intriguing files were noted.

One in particular is of considerable interest. It concerns the application of Samuel Samuels, formerly Dmitrovski, of 3 Hopefield Avenue, Belfast, for naturalisation.[17] To begin with a public notice was placed in the *Northern Whig* newspaper on 26 May 1927 which set forth that

Samuel Samuels was applying for naturalisation and that if anyone had any objections to this they should contact the Home Office. With no objections having been received, police enquiries were conducted into Samuel Samuels' background. A report was prepared which reads like a detailed CV of the man and his family.

Samuel Dmitrovski was born in Kamentetz Litovsk, Poland, on 20 October 1874, to Russian parents, Hirch and Fage Dmitrovski. Samuel arrived in Northern Ireland on 15 August 1910 with no documents. He adopted the name Samuel Samuels and the family was now known by that name. He was described as being of 'good character and loyal'. He could speak, read and write English, Hebrew and Jeagon. He intended to reside in the British Dominions for the remainder of his life and would, if called upon, enter the service of the crown. His application for naturalisation was for business reasons. He had two daughters married to British subjects and a third was soon (November 1927) to marry another, Emanuel Ryness of Glasgow.

His residences in Northern Ireland since arrival had been:

169 North St, 1910–11
19 Carlisle St, September 1911–13
32 Carlisle St,1913–15
10 Antrim Rd,1915–21
3 Hopefield Ave 1921–to date

He was a retail draper – the owner of five establishments. He had two sons and six daughters, all of whom had been born in Poland. Samuel married in March 1893 (initially this was incorrectly given as 1903) at Puzanna, Poland. His wife was Polish. Still at home were his daughters: Polly (born 1907), Annie (born June 1909), Leah and Esther. All the birth certificates had been destroyed in Poland. His sons Leon and Joseph Dmitrovski were to apply for naturalisation also. Naturalisation was granted to Samuel Samuels on 30 July 1928.

A file from 1931 concerns the application by Rabbi Schachter to employ Gerson Sungalowsky, a Lithuanian Jew then living in Belgium, as the reader, ritual slaughterer and circumcisor to the Belfast Hebrew congregation.[18] There was a considerable amount of prevarication on the part of the authorities over this application and when Sungalowsky was allowed to move to Belfast he left after three weeks. Another file in this collection, covering the period 1923–5, relates to the imprisonment for larceny of Jacob Harris, a Russian from Livonia, and the arrangements for his deportation.[19] Further careful research in this archive should reveal more references to Jewish individuals and families in Belfast in this period.

CONCLUSION

Through studying the genealogy of Jewish men and women from a variety of backgrounds and classes we can see the diversity of this small community over a century of change and in doing so chart the changes and developments of society collectively and the Jewish community in particular. It is important that in what is eventually becoming a multicultural and more diverse society that we do not forget just how peculiar and fascinating the presence of German, Russian and Polish Jewish families would have initially appeared to the working class men and women of north Belfast, who in all reality had limited experience of other cultures or nationalities. The presence of the Jewish pedlar, carpenter, draper, glazier, baker, tailor, traveller, jeweller or even Rabbi[20] must have had a remarkable effect on broadening the cultural horizons of Belfast's indigenous residents. This subject of Jewish experience in Belfast's Protestant and Catholic ghettos needs much more research, and quickly before the spoken recollections of a past generation is forgotten.

We have not provided many answers to questions about the social composition of the Jewish community in Northern Ireland, but have rather outlined the building blocks that are available to do so. Using the sources highlighted in this essay, it ought to be possible to build up a more detailed picture of this community from the middle of the nineteenth century. Much work needs to be done before we have a fuller understanding and a more informed appreciation of the contribution of the Jewish community to life in Northern Ireland at both the economic and social level, not to mention the religious, political and cultural dimensions. We hope there will be those who will be stimulated to take this up.

ACKNOWLEDGEMENTS

We are grateful to members of the Jewish community for assistance in the research and writing of this article. In particular Steven Jaffe and Stuart Rosenblatt were enormously helpful. Steven Jaffe is currently writing a history of the Jewish community in Northern Ireland. Stuart Rosenblatt is the founder of the Irish Jewish Genealogical Society and has computerised over 33,000 records relating to Jewish people in Ireland.

NOTES

1 *Linen Hall Newsletter*, no. 22, November 2004, p. 7.
2 Cecil Roth, *Encyclopaedia Judaica*, p. 5; Harold Ross, *History of the Jews in Ireland* (privately published, no date).
3 Harold Ross, *op. cit.*
4 Louis Hyman, *The Jews of Ireland: from Earliest Times to the Year 1910* (Shannon, 1972), p. 208.
5 *Jewish Encyclopedia VII.*
6 Hyman, *op. cit.*, p. 208; Bernard Shillman, *A Short History of the Jews in Ireland* (Dublin, 1945).
7 Hyman, *op. cit.*, p. 208.
8 Dermot Keogh, *Jews in Twentieth Century Ireland* (Cork, 1998), p. 69.
9 The Ulster Historical Foundation has a database of these marriages.
10 PRONI SCH/240/1/1–2.
11 The Public Record Office of Northern Ireland has records of over 1,500 national schools in Northern Ireland. An index of the schools covered is available to aid the researcher.
12 PRONI LA/7/11AB/2, Minutes of the Cemetery Committee of the Belfast Corporation, 1867–87.
13 PRONI T/1602/1.
14 See www.historyfromheadstones.com for a case study of the Jewish quarter at Belfast City Cemetery by Pamela McIlveen (or Linden as she was then).
15 PRONI LA/59/2F/6, Belfast Rural District Council minutes.
16 Cecil Roth, *op. cit.*, p. 760.
17 PRONI HA/5/1447.
18 PRONI HA/5/795.
19 PRONI HA/5/779.
20 Michael Leinkram aged 48, Rabbi, born Austria. (1901 census for Bristol Street, Belfast, National Archives of Ireland, ref A93/8).

Nomenclature for Ulster emigrants

Scotch-Irish or Scots-Irish?

MICHAEL MONTGOMERY

IN THE SUMMER OF 1995 I had the opportunity to say a few words at the launch of *The Scots-Irish in the Hills of Tennessee*, a book by Northern Ireland journalist Billy Kennedy at the office of his newspaper, the *Newsletter*.[1] As a native of the hills about which Kennedy wrote and as someone quite interested in connections (especially with respect to speech[2]) between my part of the world and the one I was visiting, I pointed out several historical links and commonalities between Tennessee and the historical province of Ulster. At a reception following the formalities, however, I was surprised when a local man approached and chided me (and my compatriots) for using *Scotch-Irish* to refer to Americans whose ancestors came from Ulster. '*Scots-Irish* is the correct term', he insisted. 'Remember, Scotch is the drink, Scots are the people'. Having grown up acquainted with only *Scotch-Irish*, I was rather puzzled. In the first forty-five years of my experience in Tennessee and elsewhere in the American South, *Scotch-Irish* was a perfectly neutral and respectable term, one used without negative connotations and never suggesting an alcoholic beverage. It was the exclusive term employed by my family of abstainers, my relatives, and many others I was aware of, whether they claimed Ulster ancestry or not. Even if it did little but account for our minority-group status as Presbyterians in an ocean of Baptists, our 'Scotch-Irishness' was an uncontroversial, indeed uncommented-upon, fact of life and our family history.

After the title of Kennedy's book and the admonition at his launch prompted me to pay attention, I began noticing *Scots-Irish*. As shown by papers delivered at academic conferences (such as biennial Ulster-American Heritage Symposia) and other events, it has gained some currency against *Scotch-Irish* in scholarly circles and among genealogists, presumably not because such people are teetotallers so much as in recognition of usage in the British Isles, where today people in Scotland are called *Scots* rather than *Scotch* (an issue to which I return below). By almost any measure, however, *Scotch-Irish* remains the more widely used term in the United States. While two books recently published there have promoted the use of *Scots-Irish* (i.e., *The People with No Name: Ireland's Ulster Scots, America's Scots Irish and the Creation of a British Atlantic World, 1689-1764* and *Born Fighting: How the Scots Irish Shaped America*), published titles with *Scotch-Irish* have always been and continue to be far more numerous.[3] This can be seen by the holdings in any American library. For example, the online catalogue of the Library of Congress lists sixty-four books with *Scotch-Irish* in their main title, but only four with *Scots-Irish*, while at a regional history library in Knoxville, Tennessee, the ratio of titles is forty-eight to seven (six with *Scots-Irish* are by Billy Kennedy). In many other ways the dominance of *Scotch-Irish* in the United States can be demonstrated.[4]

Since the history and application of *Scotch-Irish* are covered in detail elsewhere, this essay will recount little of that discussion, even though misinformation and misunderstanding about the term and the people to whom it refers remain prevalent.[5] As discussed below, *Scotch-Irish* has changed in meaning since its first documented use in the sixteenth century, when it referred to Gaelic-speakers from western Scotland. When it appeared in America, the label was restricted to Ulster emigrants of Presbyterian heritage who spoke English or Scots. Beginning around the end of the nineteenth century, the term widened to encompass other Protestants (Anglicans, Quakers, etc.) and eventually, for some writers, to Ulster emigrants collectively, because they were presumed to have assimilated the dominant Scottish-based culture of Ulster (in Ireland *Ulster Scot* seems to have undergone a similar expansion in meaning in the twentieth century).[6]

The distinctiveness, real or perceived, of the Ulster emigrant stream to colonial North America has been much debated and is an issue on which terminology from the eighteenth century can throw interesting and perhaps instructive light.[7] This paper hopes to inform this issue and bring some clarity to whether *Scotch-Irish* or *Scots-Irish* is more appropriate, historically or otherwise, by citing early examples of these terms and considering objections to both terms. Citations from the seventeenth and eighteenth century are crucial to ascertaining their historicity and usage, but they cannot by themselves reveal the full or precise dimensions of the cultural identity of a group of people in Ulster or colonial America as articulated by either themselves or others. Issues of 'identity' in Ireland are complex and often contentious and indeed have been so for a long time. Identities are often treated as little more than labels for static, simplistic, dichotomous categories. An American can easily misstep in dealing with matters of cultural identity in Ireland. In Ulster particularly these are often multiple, overlapping, and fluid, and I will henceforth eschew the subject. As Estyn Evans reminded us years ago, evidence from the historical record 'cannot fully illuminate the largely unwritten processes of cultural adaptation that are involved in the task of colonisation, whether in the initial settlements or, particularly, in the [American] backwoods'.[8] This observation is certainly true with respect to group names.

In Britain *Scotch-Irish*/*Scots-Irish* is first documented referring to Scottish Highlanders and Islanders, who for centuries had moved back and forth to the Antrim coast and who in Elizabethan times threatened the stability of English rule in Ulster. The sea-based territory spanning the North Channel, especially the lands dominated by the powerful MacDonnell clan, formed a zone of influence distinct from the rest of Ireland. In a letter of 14 April 1573, Elizabeth I stated, 'We are given to understand that a nobleman named "Sorley Boy" [MacDonnell] and others, who be of the Scotch-Irish race, and some of the wild Irish, at this time are content to acknowledge our true and mere right to the countrie of Ulster and the crowne of Ireland', and in the same document she contrasted the 'meer Irish' with the 'Scotch-Irish'.[9] This sense of *Scotch-Irish* persisted for more than a century, as is evident from a statement *c.*1700 from Scottish court proceedings: 'Thir [i.e., those] of

Birkay, the Irische men and our Scottis Irishe, acknawledge the same for thair first and mother toung ... commounlie ... called ... the Gathelik toung'.[10] How widely this sense of *Scotch-Irish* was known in seventeenth-century Scotland can hardly be guessed from only two citations, but three further ones recently put on the record by Young are quite relevant and provocative:

> [Margaret Sime was] ane uther Scottis Irish gentlewoman' (1643, Elgin kirk session records)
>
> Indorsed: Esquire Uptun petitione desiring warrant to raise a regiment of Scots Irisihes in Scotland' (1689, as quoted from William Fraser, *The Melvilles*, iii, 217)
>
> [E]very fifth man in the English forces was either of this nation, or Scots-Irish, a people of the same blood with us'. (*c.* 1688, in Andrew Fletcher, *Political Works*)[11]

Young suggests that all three refer to Presbyterians from Ulster, in the first case to a refugee from the Irish Rebellion of 1641–2 who was displaced to north-east Scotland and needed assistance. Such an interpretation seems less likely for the other two cases, which at least as plausibly referred to folk from Gaelic-speaking Scotland. Indeed, it is possible that the same interpretation holds for the 1643 example, as Gaelic was known to be spoken in parts of Morayshire near Elgin at the end of the seventeenth century.[12] Interestingly, no instances of *Scotch-Irish* or *Scots-Irish* from seventeenth-century Ireland have surfaced to date.

What is fascinating is that at the very same time that *Scotch-Irish* was being applied in Scotland to one group of people, it appeared in North America for Presbyterian colonists from Ulster, the earliest example being from a Maryland affidavit in 1689/90:

> I William Pattent was at worke at James Minders and one night as I was at worke Mr Matt: Scarbrough came into the house of sd Minders and sett down by me as I was at work, the sd Minder askt him if he came afoot, he made answer again and sd he did, saying that man, meaning me, calling me Rogue makes me goe afoot, also makes it his business to goe from house to house to ruinate me, my Wife and Children for ever. I made answer is it I Mr.Scarbrough[?] and he

> replyed and said ay you, you Rogue, for which doing ile whip you and make my Wife whipp to whipp you, and I answered if ever I have abused [you] at any time, or to any bodies hearing, I will give you full satisfaction to your own Content. [At which Scarbrough said] You Scotch Irish dogg it was you, with that he gave me a blow on the face saying it was no more sin to kill me then to kill a dogg, or any Scotch Irish dogg, giving me another blow in the face. now saying goe to yr god that Rogue and have a warrant for me and I will answer it. Wm.Patent[.]' (from an affidavit recorded on 15 March 1689/90 in Somerset County, Maryland, in a hearing to bring charges against Matthew Scarbrough)[13]

Before examining further American quotations, it may be useful to consider a wider context for the term *Scotch-Irish*. In the American colonial period a large number of people, in both relative and raw terms, left Ulster for North America, most noticeably from the second decade of the eighteenth century. Exactly how many has been debated for over a century. One early historian argued for more than a third of a million,[14] while more recent economic historians have proposed lower figures (Dickson, for example, based his estimate of 130,000 on the tonnage of passenger ships known to have left Ulster ports for America).[15] The competing criteria used for such estimates make for an engaging subject in itself, but suffice it to say that the most recent statement on the issue, and perhaps the most authoritative one to date, is that at least 150,000 natives of Ulster arrived in American colonies prior to the outbreak of the American Revolution in 1776.[16] According to one historian, 'their migration represented the single largest movement of any group from the British Isles to British North America during the eighteenth century'.[17]

The history of the term *Scotch-Irish* has been poorly understood by some and a matter of contention for others. It is sometimes said to be a designation that arose in the late nineteenth century. Rehder, for example, stated that 'it was not until much later [than arrival in America] that they would become known as the Scotch-Irish people'.[18] According to this view, *Scotch-Irish* was popularised by Protestant descendants of emigrants from Ulster to promote a history separate from that of Catholic Irish arriving in greater numbers on American shores from the early years of the nineteenth century, particularly the 1840s, and that the term was a product of ethnic and religious hostility and prejudice. Perhaps the strongest advocate of this idea was Michael J. O'Brien, director of the American Irish Historical Society in the early twentieth century, who published prolifically on early emigrants from Ireland to North America. He attributed *Scotch-Irish* to 'anti-Irish propaganda' and argued that many American Protestants who espoused the label were unaware that they had Catholic ancestors either in the United States or in Ireland. 'Nor', he believed, 'can we find in the official records any reference to the "Scotch-Irish", for in all written documents of the Colonial period, where the immigrants from Ireland are mentioned at all, they are referred to invariably by their proper racial designation [ie, simply as Irish]'.[19] In another essay O'Brien even alleged that Americans whose ancestors came from Scotland had invented *Scotch-Irish* to appropriate a heritage that rightfully belonged to Ireland (he would have rejected *Scots-Irish* with equal vigor).[20] Whether because others have been slow or less public to counter the idea, in the field of American history one often finds the belief that *Scotch-Irish* lacks legitimacy because of its alleged political motivation and that both *Scotch-Irish* and *Scots-Irish* are suspect because they are said to have been rare in the eighteenth century and not used by Ulster emigrants themselves. According to Griffin, Ulster Presbyterian emigrants were distinctive, if for no other reason, in that they had 'no name': 'Referring to themselves simply as "frontier inhabitants", Ulster's Presbyterian migrants had a better idea of what they were not than what they were'.[21] However, from the historical record presented in part here, it would seem more accurate to judge that there were several names such emigrants went by, and it is in the variety of labels applied to these people that they are arguably most distinctive.

It is indisputable that the currency of *Scotch-Irish* increased greatly in the United States toward the end of the nineteenth century, for political and social reasons beyond the scope of this essay to treat.[22] However, this fact should not obscure or override the earlier history of the term, to which we now return. As already suggested, historians have to date believed that *Scotch-Irish* was at best infrequent in colonial America. According to Leyburn, whose volume is still an authority on the subject and who provided heretofore the most comprehensive discussion of names for Ulster emigrants in the pre-Revolutionary era, 'when they began to come to America, most colonial officials and others who had occasion to mention [Ulster Presbyterian emigrants] referred to them as Irish. sometimes varying this term with "Ulster-Irish" or "Northern Irish", or "Irish Presbyterians"' and further that 'there is no way of ascertaining how readily the name was accepted or applied in each of the colonies'.[23] Leyburn's assessment reflects the fact that collectively he and two other authors could find only nine instances of *Scotch-Irish* from the colonial period (two of which were from Britain).[24]

However, Leyburn and other scholars did not do their prospecting as well as they might have done. Over the years the present writer has, with the assistance of colleagues, collected many further instances from seventeenth- and eighteenth-century America. The list, which includes twenty-four examples of *Scotch-Irish* and three of *Scots-Irish*[25], is three times as long as that amassed by Leyburn and others. So far as can be determined, in that period the labels always referred to Presbyterian settlers. In most cases they were used by outsiders (usually colonial officials of one kind or another), but one of them, by a Church of England clergyman, noted that *Scotch-Irish* was a term of self-reference:

> The first settlers of this county were for the far greatest part originally English, but of the late number of years Irish (who usually call themselves Scotch-Irish) have transplanted themselves and their families from the north of Ireland (1723, Rev. William Beckett, Church of England clergyman, Lewes, Delaware)[26]

What is particularly striking about *Scotch-Irish* and *Scots-Irish* in eighteenth-century America is the diversity of people who used it. Taken together, examples from these commentators imply that the term *Scotch-Irish*, at least, was widely understood, even if not actually found quite often in the written record. A significant example appeared in a 1737 issue of the *Virginia Gazette*, whose editor said the following in a preface to an open letter by an emigrant writing home to a Presbyterian pastor back in County Tyrone:

> We hear from *Pennsylvania*, That several Ships have arriv'd there, and in the Three Lower Counties, within a few Weeks past, from the North of *Ireland*, and from *Holland*, and have brought a great Number of *Irish*, *Scotch-Irish*, and *Palatines*, Passengers.[27]

Perhaps what is most significant about this example is its appearance in a newspaper that was circulated widely in Virginia and neighbouring colonies. Its anonymous editor could have used *Scotch-Irish* without comment only if it had been immediately interpretable and unambiguous to a broad readership, so it must have had considerable currency in the American colonies by 1737.

Around the same time, the Scotsman Alexander Hamilton (1712–56) recorded in his diary of 25 August, 1744:

> I dined att Williams att Stonington [Connecticut] with a Boston merchant named Gardiner and one Boyd, a Scotch Irish pedlar. The pedlar seemed to understand his business to a hair. He sold some dear bargains to Mrs. Williams, and while he smoothed her up with palaber, the Bostonian amused her with religious cant.[28]

This use of the term by a native of Scotland suggests that Hamilton regarded the pedlar as belonging to a group distinct from both the Scots and the Irish.

Telling quotes come from Charles Woodmason, the Anglican clergyman assigned to the interior of South Carolina in the 1760s. With regard to the Chief Justice of the colony, he stated that 'altho' he was a Gentleman of Ireland, yet he abominated these Northern Scotch Irish and they are certainly the worst Vermin on Earth' in a private journal written for either himself or fellow churchmen back in England.[29] Woodmason also referred to the group as *Scots-Irish*:

> Such a Pack I never met with—Neither English, Scots Irish, or Carolinian by Birth—Neither of one Church or other nor of any denomination by Profession, not having (like some of the Lynchs Creek people) ever seen a Minister[.][30]

The use of the two terms by an English clergyman recently dispatched to South Carolina, suggests that both must have been familiar in the mother country as well as in the colonies.

Like examples from Pattent and Woodmason above, a number of

examples show that *Scotch-Irish* was often used with pejorative connotations[31]:

> In case [the Swiss] should fail me a second time, I will endeavor to supply there places with Scots Irish from Pennsylvania, who flock over thither in such numbers, that there is not elbow room for them. They swarm like the Goths and Vandals of old & will over-spread our Continent soon. (1736, William Byrd, Virginia)[32]

> Whereas some ill-disposed Persons, regardless of Truth and Honor, have industriously spread a Report very detrimental as well to the private Reputation, as Publick Character, of NATHANIEL GRUBB, one of the Members of the House of Assembly of this Province, asserting that the said Nathaniel, being informed that sundry of the Back Inhabitants were cut off, and destroyed by our savage Enemies, replied, "That there were only some Scotch-Irish kill'd, who could well be spared …" (1756, *Pennsylvania Gazette*)[33]

But quite clearly others were not derogatory, including the following:

> They are a colony from Pennsylvania of what we call Scotch Irish Presbyterians who with others in neighboring Tracts had settled together in order to have a teacher, i.e., a minister of their own opinion and choice. (1755, Arthur Dobbs, Governor of North Carolina)[34]

> On the Conewana-Creek, is another Settlement of the Scotch Irish … (1771, Philip Fithian, tutor in Virginia)[35]

Next to a Presbyterianism religious affiliation *Scotch-Irish* was most often used in the colonial period in reference to speech habits, both to emigrants from Ulster and to those, including a runaway slave, who apparently learned such habits from Ulster emigrants:

> I ought perhaps to except [from the universal prevalence of dialect] the United States of America, in which dialect is hardly known; unless some scanty remains of the croaking, gutteral idioms of the Dutch, still observable in New York; the Scotch-Irish, as it used to be called, in some of the back settlers of the Middle States; and the whining, canting drawl brought by some republican, Oliverian and Puritan emigrants from the West of England, and still kept up by their unregenerated descendants of New England – may still be called dialects … (1800, Jonathan Boucher, Maryland)[36]

> RUN away from the Subscriber, on the 16th Instant, a likely Negro Fellow named JACOB ... He was born in *Pennsylvania*, bred a Farmer, pretends to great Skill in Farriery, speaks in the *Scotch-Irish* dialect, and in conversation frequently uses the Words *moreover* and *likewise.* (1776, *Virginia Gazette*)[37]

From the range of fore-going examples from a large geographical territory in the seventeenth and eighteenth centuries, it appears not only that *Scotch-Irish* was a more established term than reported in the literature to date, but, just as important, that it was one whose usage defies several generalisations made about it in the past. Citations indicate that, while some settlers found the label offensive, others accepted *Scotch-Irish* often without protest, meaning that they must have viewed the term as a neutral descriptor. Whether those who used or accepted *Scotch-Irish* thought that the people to whom it referred were any less Irish is not easy to determine.

While *Scotch-Irish* was certainly cultivated in the nineteenth century by descendants of Protestants to emphasise their Protestantism, this hardly means that it was used only in this way. In his autobiography written in the 1870s, Dr J.G.M. Ramsey, an early Tennessee historian and founder of the East Tennessee Historical Society, wrote: 'My paternal grandfather was Reynolds Ramsey. It is believed that his parents were Scotch-Irish Presbyterians, and that his father on coming to America settled at New-Castle, Delaware'.[38] It seems unlikely that Ramsey was here using the term in any sense other than an objective one for a person of Presbyterian heritage whose ancestors came from Ireland. *Scotch-Irish* may have been used elsewhere by some, particularly in eastern cities, to avoid the label *Irish*, but as a neutral term it must historically have had, as it still has, considerable currency in places like East Tennessee and the American interior and to have been used matter of factly.[39]

On this basis and also given the earlier record, it is unreasonable either to dismiss an established term in good standing for many generations in many parts of the United States because some may have used it to express prejudice or to substitute instead *Scots-Irish*, which has much inferior support and justification historically. *Scotch-Irish* has continued to be sanctioned by authoritative reference volumes like *Harvard Encyclopedia of American Ethnic Groups* and *American*

Immigrant Cultures: Builders of a Nation.[40] Both have an entry on the *Scotch-Irish* and use this term to designate the eighteenth-century, mainly Presbyterian emigrant stream from Ulster. As far as the field of genealogy is concerned, one notes the pertinent electronic discussion list named Scotch-Irish-L@rootsweb.com (there is no Scots-Irish-L). The Scotch-Irish Society of the United States of America, founded in 1889, has a number of state chapters and publishes an annual journal, the *Journal of Scotch-Irish Studies.* There is no Scots-Irish Society.

It has sometimes been stated on both sides of the Atlantic that *Scotch-Irish* and *Scots-Irish* are solely American terms, unknown in the British Isles and that for this reason they are said to be inappropriate for people who originated in Ireland[41] (Leyburn, for example, concluded that 'the name "Scotch-Irish" is unknown in Ulster, the northern province of Ireland, from which the Scotch-Irish came').[42] Implicit in this claim is that Americans have misconstrued the history of Ireland and have devised a term for a people not recognised in the old country. I have already shown that some of those who used *Scotch-Irish* in the eighteenth century were not born in America. Although we can never be certain, it seems unlikely that all of them would have picked up the term only after arriving there. More recent is the work of scholars in Northern Ireland, some of whom were contemporaries of Leyburn, but of whom he seems to have been unaware. Ethnologist Estyn Evans and historian Maldwyn Jones, two Welshmen, have both used *Scotch-Irish* in important twentieth-century scholarship.[43] Robert Gregg, the founder of modern Ulster-Scots studies and a native of Larne, County Antrim, employed 'Scotch-Irish dialect' in his work on Ulster speech, as did John Braidwood, who stated that 'the Scots tradition is so much the dominant one that many erroneously equate it with the Ulster Dialect, and regard all Ulstermen as Scotch Irish'.[44] One might argue that Evans and Jones were writing about settlers in America and used *Scotch-Irish* in deference to established convention there. But Gregg and Braidwood, two linguists, were not. Thus, at least in Northern Ireland academic circles, *Scotch-Irish* has been a familiar usage.

It is sometimes argued that, whatever its currency in the past, *Scotch-Irish* is inappropriate because people in Scotland now call themselves

Scots, not *Scotch*, and some people in Ulster call themselves *Ulster Scots*. This view has in part motivated the adoption of *Scots-Irish*. Let us examine these assertions. While it is true that many – probably most – in Scotland today apply *Scots* to themselves and to the language they speak (a close relative to English) and that this usage is frequent in writing and in middle class speech, a closer look at the history of *Scots* and related forms is revealing. The on-line *Dictionary of the Scots Language* lists a staggering twenty-nine orthographic variants used before 1700, but the four forms of primary interest here (and historically the most prevalent) are *Scottis*, *Scottish*, *Scotch*, and *Scots*.[45] Given this diversity and that their histories overlap, our discussion must be simplified somewhat.

Scottis dates from 1375 and was the most common form in Scotland until the seventeenth century. It parallels the English form *Scottish* in the same manner that the Scots form *Inglis* parallels the English one *English*. At a point impossible to determine, but most likely in the sixteenth century, *Scottis* became contracted to *Scots* and thus pronounced as one syllable. *Scottish* was the historic form in England and dates from as early as 900. It was likewise reduced to one syllable, i.e. *Scotch*, a form not attested in the written record in England before 1570 but probably representing a somewhat older pronunciation. As part of the Anglicising influence on Scottish culture and the Scots language, *Scotch* entered Scotland in the mid seventeenth century and became dominant there in the eighteenth century. In Scotland *Scotch* has long been felt, quite accurately, to be an English form. This idea supported its usage when Scots were keen to follow English models, as they were in the eighteenth century in rooting out 'barbarous Scotticisms' from their speech. But in the nineteenth century *Scotch* began falling into disfavour in some circles, so much so that many in Scotland now consider its use patronising. Today it is quite often avoided in favour of *Scots*, which is felt to be more authentic, descended from the earlier form *Scottis*. In the early nineteenth century Sir Walter Scott preferred *Scots* for its antiquity, stating that 'Scotch must be spelled Scots to keep up the orthography of the antique age', a view that says more about his nostalgia than about usage in his day (after all, he would not have advised against *Scotch* if it had not been prevalent).[46]

Whatever the attitudes against *Scotch* may be in Scotland today, it penetrated the speech of the country deeply and remains a subject of periodic and sometimes passionate comment. Writing in the first issue of *Scotia: The Journal of the St. Andrew Society* in 1907, the editor addressed the terminological issue of whether the publication would use the adjective *Scotch*, *Scottish*, or *Scots*. While granting that 'in the opinion of my colleagues, the adjective "Scotch" and its compounds "Scotchman" and "Scotchwoman", are essentially un-Scottish, and altogether to be avoided' and that 'of late years there has been a growing tendency to use "Scots"', the editor had 'always regarded [this] as simply a literary renascence; I might almost say an affectation. My strong conviction is that the great majority of my fellow-countrymen habitually employ "Scotch-man" and "Scotch" in their daily conversation; occasionally varied by the use of "Scottish" in more familiar and homely associations'.[47] Further, the *Concise Scots Dictionary* (s.v. *Scots* A) cites *Scotch* as 'still the regular vernacular form' in the latter half of the twentieth century.[48] So *Scotch* has by no means disappeared in Scotland. What is most important for us is that *Scotch* was well-nigh universal in Britain and Ireland in the eighteenth century, making it the form that emigrated to America and became the natural basis for the compound noun *Scotch-Irish*. This is why during that period *Scottish-Irish* was unknown and *Scots-Irish* was much less frequent than *Scotch-Irish*.

What about Ulster? *Scotch* was the principal form there too, and *Scots* was rare until well into the nineteenth century (the compound *Ulster Scot(s)* apparently dates from around 1870[49]). For example, the 1838 Ordnance Survey memoir for the parish of Templepatrick in south-west Antrim reported that 'a great portion of [the inhabitants] are of Scotch origin and they all have a good deal of Scotch manner and accent'.[50] In 1880 a compiler of traditional Antrim and Down vocabulary stated that 'in some districts in the east of the two counties people still talk a Scotch dialect, but with a modified Scotch accent; the old people talk more "broadly" than the young'[51], and at the turn of the twentieth century, Donegal men hiring themselves out as farm workers spoke of 'going up till the Lag[g]an, to lift the Scotch', i.e. to learn English.[52]

Even today *Scots* is not the traditional term in rural Ulster, where *Scotch* is the form used in reference to people and to their form of speech. This fact is recognised by the names Ulster-Scotch Leid Societie and Boord o Ulster-Scotch, also known by their formal English equivalents, Ulster-Scots Language Society and Ulster-Scots Agency. In that *Scots* is the more recent term in both Scotland and Ireland, we see that the gentleman who confronted me at the book reception was not in touch with his own background or with the Ulster countryside. Or perhaps he did not appreciate that *Scotch-Irish* refers to an American group, that it is the term generally used in the United States, and that Americans have a right and a prerogative to refer to the group in whatever manner they might see fit. He was certainly not alone in preferring *Scots-Irish*, the form that, for whatever reason, seems more and more the usual one in Northern Ireland. Popularised perhaps by Rory Fitzpatrick's Ulster Television series and accompanying book *God's Frontiersmen: The Scots-Irish Epic* in 1989, this preference is reflected in other retellings of the story of Ulster emigration to America such as in the books of Kennedy (seven titles to date), the *On Eagle's Wing* musical drama that debuted in Belfast in May 2004, and the Chistera Films documentary for BBC TV scheduled for transmission January 2005.[53] Usage in Northern Ireland remains divided, however. The on-line archive of the *Irish News* (from 1996–2004) contains fifty-four items employing *Scots-Irish* and twenty-nine that have *Scotch-Irish*. Neither that newspaper nor the *Belfast Telegraph* seems to follow a standard practice for either spelling or definition (in both papers the two terms occasionally refer to people in Ulster who are otherwise known as *Ulster Scots*). *The Ulster-Scot*, the occasional paper produced by the Ulster-Scots Agency, normally uses *Scots-Irish*, but reprints material from other publications having *Scotch-Irish*; it also uses both *Ulster-Scots* and *Ulster-Scotch*.

The dictum that *Scotch* is proper usage only for the drink seems sometimes to have approached the status of a mantra, and this view has moved well beyond the realm of teetotalers and those of religious sensitivity on the issue, though rarely in print (Kennedy is an exception, stating that because of the association *Scotch-Irish* 'causes offence' to many on both sides of the Atlantic[54]). Might Americans not naturally be offended that people elsewhere feel compelled to impose their practice on Americans? The historical status of *Scotch* or *Scotch-Irish* to refer to people and the priority of American usage seem not to matter to those holding this view, which is essentially one of political correctness, nor does the fallacious assumption that a term can or should be restricted to only one meaning. *Irish* refers to both a people and a language, as do countless other terms. If *Scotch* is to be reserved for only the drink and to be replaced in compound nouns whose centuries-long history can be documented, by this logic we should eat *Scots broth* and *butterscots candy*, and Americans should use *Scots tape* (i.e., *Scotch tape*, what is called *cellotape* in Britain and Ireland). Except in rare or deliberate cases, context indicates which meaning of a word is appropriate in a particular instance. *Scotch* is rarely ambiguous.

Thus, several reasons and factors legitimate and favour *Scotch-Irish*. It has been used for more than three centuries and has precedence over and a better claim as a historical term than *Scots-Irish*. It had considerable currency before the late nineteenth century and was more prevalent in the colonial period than Leyburn suspected. Further digging into the record may produce even more reason to question his belief that his few citations 'practically complete the colonial list'.[55] *Scotch* has been the traditional term for people of Scottish ancestry or tradition in both Ulster and Scotland and to some extent is still used. Logical reasons to avoid *Scotch-Irish* are hard to find.

Perhaps no consideration matters more than a final one. This concerns the privilege, granted routinely to groups in modern society, to name themselves. Descendants of Ulster emigrants call themselves as well as their ancestors *Scotch-Irish*. However much historians might favour a particular name, their views would seem inadequate, even misguided, if they conflict with those who identify with a group in question. Few would argue that Americans of African descent do not have the right to call themselves African-Americans, as they have increasingly chosen to do, and that choice is now recognised in common discourse. Though they do not form an analogous group in some ways, why should Americans of Ulster ancestry be treated any differently? The Scotch-Irish were not confined to only the eighteenth century stage. It would be interesting to know which writers about Ulster emigrants have surveyed people having such ancestry about nomenclature.

Readers will have noticed that this essay has taken a more polemical edge and have probably realised long since that the choice between *Scotch-Irish* and *Scots-Irish* involves in one sense a minuscule issue, the pronunciation of a single consonant. But names are birthrights not granted to others to judge or choose. Americans do not look abroad for the authority on how to speak English, so why should they do so regarding what to label themselves? *Scotch-Irish* has been the dominant usage in American circles for more than three hundred years, especially by people of Presbyterian heritage with Ulster foreparents, and for this reason it should be considered the proper and correct term.

The granting of respect is one thing. If history matters, as would certainly seem to be the case for those concerned with the settlement of America, the importance of the eighteenth century for Ulster emigration can hardly be overstated. An understanding of *Scotch-Irish* from only its usage in the nineteenth century is myopic at best. Today it remains the more familiar, preferred term for countless Americans and *Scotch-Irish* has formed part of family lore for many who, if they know nothing else about their ancestry, have learned from older relatives that they are *Scotch-Irish*. Documenting the nomenclature surrounding them is part of the larger project of reconstructing who their ancestors were and who they are.

NOTES

1 Billy Kennedy, *The Scots-Irish in the Hills of Tennessee* (Londonderry, Northern Ireland, Causeway, 1995). For supplying citations of *Scotch-Irish* to him, the author gratefully acknowledges Michael Scoggins, Richard MacMaster, and Warren Hofstra.

2 See Michael Montgomery, 'How Scotch-Irish is Your English?' *Journal of East Tennessee History* 67, 1995, 1–33; Michael Montgomery, 'The Scotch-Irish Influence on Appalachian English: How Broad? How Deep?' in Curtis Wood and Tyler Blethen (eds) *Ulster and North America: Transatlantic Perspectives on the Scotch-Irish* (Tuscaloosa, University of Alabama Press, 1997).

3 Patrick Griffin, *The People with No Name: Ireland's Ulster Scots, America's Scots Irish and the Creation of a British Atlantic World, 1689–1764* (Princeton, Princeton University Press, 2001); James Webb, *Born Fighting: How the Scots Irish Shaped America* (New York, Broadway Books, 2004).

4 A view to the contrary is found in Kerby A. Miller *et al.*, *Irish Immigrants in the Land of Canaan: Letters and Memoirs from Colonial and Revolutionary America, 1675–1815* (New York, Oxford University Press, 2003), p. 24. They state that Ulster Presbyterian emigrants are 'most commonly known in the United States today as the Scots-Irish', but do not indicate the basis of this judgment.

5 Steve Ickringill, 'Not Just a Typographical Error', *Causeway,* Winter 1994–95, pp. 32–35. Many commentators take pains to dispute the idea that the Scotch-Irish were produced by the intermarriage of Scots and Irish; whatever lack of validity such a common view has, it can hardly be argued that the Scotch-Irish did not absorb many elements of native Irish culture and that they were not cultural hybrids.

6 The historiography on Ulster emigration is extensive and varied. Although both academic historians and popularising ones have assigned *Scotch-Irish* the core meaning of descendants of seventeenth-century Presbyterian settlers from Scotland, rarely do they state explicitly its boundaries. For the best general survey of the subject, see James G. Leyburn, *The Scotch-Irish: A Social History* (Chapel Hill, University of North Carolina Press, 1962). For the best synopsis of the scholarly literature, see Kenneth W. Keller, 'What is Distinctive about the Scotch-Irish?' in Robert D. Mitchell (ed) *Appalachian Frontiers: Settlement, Society & Development in the Preindustrial Era* (Lexington, University Press of Kentucky, 1991) and Maldwyn Jones, 'The Scotch-Irish in British America' in Bernard Bailyn and Philip D. Morgan (eds) *Strangers within the Realm: Cultural Margins in the First British Empire* (Chapel Hill, University of North Carolina Press, 1991).

7 The case for distinctiveness is most often made on the basis of religious expression, folk culture, and especially speech. For the latter, see Michael

Montgomery, 'The Many Faces of the Scotch-Irish', *Familia*, 16, 2000, pp. 24–40; Michael Montgomery, 'Eighteenth-Century Nomenclature for Ulster Emigrants', *Journal of Scotch-Irish Studies*, 2, 2001, pp. 1–6; Michael Montgomery, 'Ulster-Scots: A Language of Scotch-Irish Emigrants', *Journal of Scotch-Irish Studies*, 2, 2001, pp. 125–37; Michael Montgomery and Robert J. Gregg. 'The Scots Language in Ulster' in Charles Jones (ed) *The Edinburgh History of the Scots Language* (Edinburgh, Edinburgh University Press, 1997), pp. 569–622. Keller, *loc. cit.*, p. 85, believes that no one cultural element distinguishes the Scotch-Irish, but rather that they had a habit 'to combine a series of customs, attitudes, and institutions that became distinctive in combination, rather than in any individual component'.

8 E. Estyn Evans, 'The Scotch-Irish in the New World: An Atlantic Heritage', *Journal of the Royal Society of Antiquaries of Ireland*, 95, 1965, p. 39.

9 *Calendar of Patent and Close Rolls of Chancery*, as cited in Leyburn, *op. cit.*, p. 329.

10 H. Dalrymple, *Decisions of the Court of Sessions from 1698 to 1718*, Bell and Bradfute (ed) (Edinburgh, J. Dickson and Silvester Doig, 1792), volume 1, 73/29. See *Dictionary of the Older Scottish Tongue*, s.v. *toung*.

11 John R. Young, 'Scotland and Ulster in the Seventeenth Century: The Movement of Peoples across the North Channel' in William Kelly and John R. Young (ed) *Ulster and Scotland, 1600–2000: History, Language, and Identity* (Dublin, Four Courts, 2004), 29, 31.

12 Charles J. Withers, *Gaelic in Scotland 1698–1981: The Geographical History of a Language* (Edinburgh, Donald, 1984).

13 John Polk, 'Oldest Use of the Term Scotch-Irish in the Americas?' <http//: homepages.rootsweb.com/~merle/Articles/OldestUseSI.htm>

14 Charles A. Hanna, *The Scotch-Irish or the Scot in North Britain, North Ireland, and North America*, 2 vols (New York, Putnam, 1902).

15 R.J. Dickson, *Ulster Emigration to Colonial America 1718-1775* (London, Routledge and Kegan Paul, 1966); reprinted with a introduction by Graeme Kirkham, Belfast, Ulster Historical Foundation, 1987. In his introduction to the reprinting of Dickson's book, Kirkham suggests that 'It seems certain that some upward revision of the figures presented in *Ulster Emigration to Colonial America* will be necessary for at least part of the period' (p. xiv).

16 This was the consensus (at a meeting in Staunton, Virginia, in September 2003) of the U.S. Scholarship Panel commissioned by the Ulster American Folk Park to advise it on developing a new outdoor exhibit. This team comprised eight American academics (including several historians of emigration): Katharine Brown, Warren Hofstra, Kenneth Keller, Richard MacMaster, Kerby A. Miller, Michael Montgomery, Anita Puckett, and Marianne Wokeck. It agreed that the figure may have been much higher, but that 150,000 was a minimum figure for those coming from Ulster between 1718 and 1776 and one-half million for those coming between 1680 and 1830.

17 Griffin, *op. cit.*, p. 1.

18 John B. Rehder, 'Scotch-Irish' in David Levinson and Melvin Ember (ed) *American Immigrant Cultures: Builders of a Nation* (New York, MacMillan, 1997), pp. 767–73.
19 Michael J. O'Brien, *A Hidden Phase of American History*, 1919, p. 337. O'Brien had foremost in mind the ten volumes of the *Proceedings of the Scotch-Irish Congress* (Cincinnati, 1889–1902).
20 Michael J. O'Brien, 'The "Scotch-Irish" Myth', *Journal of the American Irish Historical Society* 24, 1925, 142–53.
21 Griffin, *op. cit.*, p. 2.
22 For commentary on this, see Kerby A. Miller, '"Scotch-Irish" Myths and "Irish" Identities in Eighteenth-Century America', in Charles Fanning (ed) *New Perspectives on the Irish Diaspora* (Carbondale, Southern Illinois University Press, 2000); Kerby A. Miller et al., *op. cit.*; Ickringill, *op cit.*
23 Leyburn, *op. cit.*, pp. 328–29, 331.
24 Leyburn, *op. cit.*, pp. 327–34; Thomas F. Hudson, 'Source of the Name Scotch-Irish' in Jack W. Weaver (ed) *Selected Proceedings of Scotch-Irish Heritage Festival, II at Winthrop College* (Charlotte, Nomad, 1984), pp. 1–10; Wayland F. Dunaway, *The Scotch-Irish in Colonial Pennsylvania* (Chapel Hill: University of North Carolina Press, 1944).
25 *Scots-Irish* was used as early as 1736 by William Byrd, 2nd of Virginia. Kennedy, *op. cit.*, p. 29ff., presents several eighteenth-century examples of *Scots-Irish*, but these are in quotations into which the author has interpolated the term for other wording in the original.
26 'The Rev. William Becket's Notices and Letters Concerning Incidents at Lewes Town, 1721–1742', *Manuscripts of the Historical Society of Pennsylvania*, p. 21.
27 Editor's preface to 'A Letter from James Murray', *Virginia Gazette*, Issue 62, September 30–October 7, 1737, p. 4.
28 Carl Bridenbaugh (ed) *A Gentleman's Progress: The Itinerarium of Dr. Alexander Hamilton, 1744* (Chapel Hill, University of North Carolina Press, 1948), p. 160.
29 Charles Woodmason, *The Carolina Back Country on the Eve of the Revolution*, ed. with an introduction by Richard J. Hooker (Chapel Hill, University of North Carolina Press, 1953), p. 50.
30 Woodmason, *op. cit.*, p. 23.
31 Griffin, *op. cit.*, p. 175 calls *Scotch-Irish* 'an eighteenth-century term of derision'.
32 William Byrd, 'Letters of the Byrd Family', *Virginia Magazine of History and Biography* 36, 1928, p. 354.
33 *Pennsylvania Gazette*, 10 June 1756.
34 R.W.D. Connor, *Race Elements in the White Population of North Carolina* (Greensboro, The College, 1920), p. 85.
35 R. G. Albion (ed) *Philip Vickers Fithian: Journal, 1770–1771* (Princeton, 1934), pp. 8–9.

36 Allen Walker Read, 'British Recognition of American Speech in the Eighteenth Century', *Dialect Notes*, 6, 1933, pp. 328.

37 *Virginia Gazette* (Purdie and Dixon), 22 March 1776.

38 W. B. Hesseltine (ed) *J. G. M. Ramsey: Autobiography and Letters* (Nashville, Tennessee Historical Commission, 1954), p. 1, reprinted with an introduction by Robert Tracy McKenzie (Knoxville, University of Tennessee Press, 2001).

39 For a study of the proportion of early Tennesseans from Ulster as opposed to from elsewhere, see Michael Montgomery and Cherel Henderson, 'Eighteenth-Century Emigrants from Ireland to Tennessee: A Report Using First Families of Tennessee Files', *Journal of East Tennessee History*, forthcoming. In an informal survey accompanying the research for this study, the authors found that from family tradition Tennesseans were, without exception, familiar with *Scotch-Irish* and not *Scots-Irish*.

40 Maldwyn Jones, 'Scotch-Irish' in Stephen Thernstrom (ed) *Harvard Encyclopedia of American Ethnic Groups* (Cambridge, Harvard University Press, 1988), pp. 895–907; Rehder, *op. cit.*

41 John Mack Faragher, 'Scotch-Irish Immigrants', in John Mack Faragher (ed) *The Encyclopedia of Colonial and Revolutionary America* (New York, Facts on File, 1990), p. 385.

42 Leyburn, *op. cit.*, p. 327.

43 E. Estyn Evans, *op. cit.*; Maldwyn Jones, 'The Scotch-Irish' in Thernstrom (ed).

44 Robert J. Gregg, 'Notes on the Phonology of a County Antrim Scotch-Irish Dialect' *Orbis* 7, 1958, pp. 392-406; Robert J. Gregg, 'Scotch-Irish Urban Speech in Ulster', in G.B. Adams (ed) *Ulster dialects: An Introductory symposium* (Holywood, Ulster Folk Museum, 1964), pp. 163–92; John Braidwood, 'The Brogue on the Tongue (Poor English–Good Irish)', *Queen's University Association Annual Report* (Belfast, Queen's University, 1977), p. 71.

45 *Dictionary of the Scots Language*, s.v. *Scots*.

46 Ibid.

47 David MacRitchie, 'The Adjectives "Scottish", "Scots", and "Scotch"', *Scotia, The Journal of the St. Andrew Society* 1, 1907, pp. 72–73.

48 Mairi Robinson *et al.* (eds) *Concise Scots dictionary* (Aberdeen, Aberdeen University Press, 1985), p. 588.

49 *Ulster Scot* was the title of a *Belfast Newsletter* column started around 1870 by the Rev. Henry Henderson. This may represent the first use of the term. I am grateful to Graham Walker for this information.

50 Angelique Day, Patrick McWilliams and Noirin Dobson (eds) *Ordnance Survey Memoirs of Ireland Volume Twenty-Six: Parishes of County Antrim X: Glynn, Inver, Kilroot, and Templecorran* (Belfast, Institute of Irish Studies, 1994), p. 106.

51 William H. Patterson, *A Glossary of Words in Use in the Counties of Antrim and Down* (London, English Dialect Society, 1880), pp. vii–viii.

52 John Braidwood, 'Ulster and Elizabethan English', in G.B. Adams (ed) *Ulster Dialects: An Introductory Symposium* (Holywood, Ulster Folk Museum, 1964), p. 35.
53 Rory Fitzpatrick, *God's Frontiersmen: The Scots-Irish Epic* (London: Weidenfeld and Nicolson, 1989).
54 Kennedy, *op. cit.*, p. 29.
55 Leyburn, *op. cit.*, p. 330.

The eighteenth-century paper-makers of the north of Ireland

ALISON MUIR

THE paper-making industry has admittedly only ever been a small part of the manufacturing economy of Ireland. Nonetheless, by the middle of the eighteenth century it had become associated with two progressive sectors of the economy – the publication of newssheets and newspapers and aspects of the linen industry and linen trade – closely enough for it to gain some significance of its own. This was achieved principally through the contributions of Francis Joy (1697–1790) and Daniel Blow (1718–1810) who would in turn become the most renowned paper-makers in the north of Ireland.

In 1737 Joy had begun a twice-weekly publication of the *Belfast News Letter* (the oldest newspaper in Europe that is still in publication). The production of the newspaper, and the newsprint required for regular distribution, was to become closely linked to his role as one of the principal paper-makers in Ulster. Recognition of his part came in the form of a grant of £200 Joy was awarded by the Irish House of Commons in Dublin in 1749. Daniel Blow, like Joy, became involved in the manufacture of paper in his capacity as a printer and stationer, and received a grant in 1750 from the Dublin Society. These awards testified to the growing recognition of the manufacture of paper. Paper-makers and merchants' advertisements of the period indicate that there was a particular demand in the linen industry for 'lapping-paper' – wrapping paper for linen cloth – though evidence of paper-wrapped linen in contemporary illustrations is curiously elusive. Often it appears that a paper-making enterprise had close links with a linen-draper's: Francis Joy and Daniel Blow themselves had interests in the growing of flax and the production of linen and sought to use the linen industry's by-products in the paper-making process. By the third quarter of the eighteenth century, therefore, Joy and Blow had become leaders of a fledgling industry which had had its slow and obscure beginnings in the generation before them and which had in turn owed much to the skills and technology brought to Ireland by Protestant refugees.

PAPER-MAKING AND TYPES OF PAPER

Paper is made from cellulosic fibrous materials. Until well into the nineteenth century, the source was worn-out textiles such as linen, hemp or cotton rags of all qualities, old sacking, sailcloth and rope. Rags were torn, sorted and carefully graded by women workers. These fibres required vigourous processing with copious amounts of water to break them down into pulp. For many centuries this processing relied on retting followed by hammers and stamping mills. The 'Hollander machine', invented in Holland in the late seventeenth century, offered a much more efficient method of beating rags and refining the pulp, and came into use throughout Europe during the eighteenth century. This is the 'engine' that Francis Joy is credited with introducing to Ulster.[1] Operation of the beating machine governed the breakdown of the fibres; this was a critical skill, crucial to the quality of the end product. The prepared pulp or 'stuff' was thinly diluted with water in a vat. A sheet of handmade paper was formed using a mould and deckle, essentially a flat rectangular sieve with a detachable rim, to hold the pulp as it was lifted in a horizontal layer from the vat; the water was then allowed to drain out. The soggy pulp sheet was laid or 'couched' onto a felt, and a pile of alternating pulp sheets and felts was built up. Two men worked as a pair: the vatman repeatedly formed uniform layers of drained pulp, and the coucher laid them – undistorted – on the felts; then the two together would screw down the press to the optimum degree to squeeze out the water and bond the fibres together to consolidate the sheet. The newly-made sheets were hung up to dry over lines in the controlled environment of a drying loft. Further pressings and maturing were required according to the quality of paper being made, as was 'sizing' – coating with gelatine to add strength and water resistance – and surface finishing processes.

The range and quality of paper made in the eighteenth century, as indeed it does today, varied considerably with its fibre sources and quality of processing, governed by its intended use. Paper falls into three broad categories of use: writing, printing and wrapping. The best quality writing and high-class printing papers were required to be white, strong and smooth – this required abundant clean water, clean white linen rags, the best equipment and highly skilled labour such as could only economically and reliably be found in regions where the tradition of fine paper-making had been long established, such as Genoa, France and Holland. This is what the Joys and Blows must have aspired to, like their Dublin counterparts. Quality of printing paper varied according to value of publication. Major Irish government publications such the *Statutes at Large* and *Journals of the House of Commons* have been found to contain paper imported from Holland supplementing the best Irish paper from the mills around Dublin.[2] Of course, a significant quantity of utilitarian paper was used for newspapers and jobbing work, which might vary from a dirty cream to range of dirty greys and blue-greys – this depended on the rags available to the mill at any given time. Coloured rags could be used to produce coloured or tinted papers; blue paper was commonly available, used for room hangings, pamphlet covers and wrapping particular goods. Old ropes, cordage and sacking made for drab and brown coloured papers of strength and durability for packaging; the dirtiest and mixed-colour rags could be added to bulk them out. Extant pieces of eighteenth-century wrapping paper such as that used by drapers for linen and shopkeepers for groceries may elude discovery, but printed ephemera such as provincial pamphlets and chapbooks, theatre bills and survivals of jobbing work provide examples of cheap printing paper.

Paper-making began in China in the first century AD and gradually spread eastwards; it was well established in southern Europe by the fourteenth century. The use of paper overtook use of parchment during the fifteenth century, while the invention and growth of printing greatly increased demand. Early demand for paper in the British Isles could be met by imports – which would always continue to provide competition for the home industry when it later developed.[3] The beginnings of the paper industries in Great Britain and Ireland appear to be characterised by the appearance of a shortlived pioneering mill many decades in advance of the industry successfully establishing itself.[4] The first mill in England appeared in 1488 but it was not until the late sixteenth century that the industry achieved a solid footing. Apart from a hint of a paper mill of 1590, paper-making did not begin in Dublin until the late seventeenth century. After initial failure, it revived during the early eighteenth century and spread to other centres in Ireland.[5] In eighteenth-century Ireland, the paper industry was one among the several regarded by economists and government as worthy of pushing in order to boost Irish manufacture. War, causing import difficulties, highlighted the need for a means of internal production, and exporting the raw material and importing the manufactured article was seen as an opportunity lost. Government-granted patents and aid, and Dublin Society premiums were aimed at encouraging various aspects of paper-making.[6] A particular difficulty in Ireland (and a concern for paper-makers anywhere) was obtaining the raw material of rags, especially clean white rags for white paper, and Dublin Society rewards were also directed towards the rag-gatherers.[7] The extent of paper-making in the north of Ireland is described here through chronicling research findings on the makers and their mills.

EARLY HISTORY OF PAPER-MAKING IN THE NORTH OF IRELAND

The first paper manufacture in Ulster was established in Dunmurry, Co. Antrim by McManus, who once lived in France, according to *The Statistical Survey of Antrim* of 1812.[8] The earliest contemporary reference is in an appendix of the *Journal of the House of Commons of Ireland*, 'To Lewis Cromlin and Denis Manesse, for a paper manufacture £103 16s', under the particulars of 'Payments made on Her Majesty's Letters, in Anno 1705'.[9] Louis Crommelin came from

Holland to Ireland in 1698, apparently at the invitation of William of Orange, to introduce improvements to the linen industry[10] and took charge of the Huguenot colony near Lisburn in Co. Antrim; he got more Protestant artisans to join him and thus a 'colony of refugees ...of many trades was soon planted at Lisburn'.[11] It seems reasonable to identify McManus/Denis Manesse with Denis Manes, a Protestant refugee from Angoulême. Denis Manes had set up paper mills in Plymouth in the 1680s and was associated with the Company of White Paper-Makers in England's mill at Southampton. From 1694 to about 1703, he was in partnership with the French entrepreneur Nicholas Dupin operating mills near Edinburgh.[12] Dupin had established a mill near Dublin in 1690, having obtained a fourteen-year patent for making white paper in Ireland (as well as setting up corporations for the manufacture of linen in England and Ireland).[13] No further reference to the Crommelin-Manes paper mill has been found. It might reasonably be surmised that it was destroyed in the fire of 1707 which consumed the whole of Lisburn town, including Crommelin's factory, in three hours. Crommelin's career continued without further reference to paper-making.

In the 1812 *Statistical Survey of County Antrim*, Dubourdieu records that the paper mill 'long since erected at Lambeg by Mr Wolfenden lasted but a short time.'[14] The Wolfenden family were Protestant refugees of Dutch extraction who settled in Lambeg in about 1685 and established various businesses, mainly as linen drapers with extensive bleach greens; later they developed a reputation for quality blanket manufacture.[15] In the *Statistical Survey of the County of Down* (1802), Dubourdieu records that, 'At Lambeg there is an extensive manufactory of papers of different kinds'.[16] Thus Dubourdieu indicates that the Wolfenden's paper mill in Co.Down, then still in existence, was preceded by a much earlier short-lived venture on the other side of the river. As the *Survey's* author Rev. John Dubourdieu was the son of the Rev. Saumaurex Dubourdieu, the cleric of the Huguenots' church in Lisburn for over 50 years and at Lambeg prior to his death in 1812, he was in a good position for local knowledge.[17]

In 1741, Richard Wolfenden, linen draper, leased 'eight acres of land and a paper mill thereon erected called part of Ballyskeagh late in lease to Abraham Wolfenden deceased'.[18] That Abraham Wolfenden had a mill is recorded in an estate rental of 1720,[19] and that he had land at Ballyskeagh is shown on an estate map of 1726.[20] This indicates that his paper mill was probably established there by 1720. Richard Wolfenden died in 1743 and the paper mill came into the possession of his son Richard. It was referred to in a lease of 1747[21] when Robert Wolfenden passed the bleach green adjoining the paper mill to the second Richard Wolfenden. In 1776, the year after the second Richard Wolfenden died, the paper mill and its contents were put up for auction:

> ... a paper mill, one of the largest in the kingdom containing 3 engines, 3 vats for making paper in with 6 presses most of them new, four with metal screws and 2 with wooden ones. Also all implements and utensils necessary for carrying on the said business in a most extensive manner with drying lofts and drying houses necessary for drying of paper. Likewise to be sold for the convenience of the purchaser a large quantity of rags most of them sorted and fit for immediate use.[22]

With three engines and three vats, it was larger than any mill in the north of Ireland in 1806 (see Table 2). It was perhaps not so much the death of the proprietor that heralded the downturn of the mill but the death in 1774 of the first master paper-maker Peter C. 'who excelled'. He was buried in Lambeg Churchyard, as were also the Wolfenden family.[23]

In 1777–8, the third Richard Wolfenden repeatedly advertised his new blanket manufacture including 'fine broad blankets in web fitting for the use of paper-makers as good as any made elsewhere';[24] this was probably complementary to, rather than in competition with, Thomas Wolfenden's established blanket business.[25] In 1779, 'the compleat furniture of paper mill consisting of double and single presses with metal screws, vats, moulds engines and the whole machinery' was offered at auction again.[26] It would appear that it remained in Wolfenden's hands, and in 1802 he advertised himself as, 'well supplied with all sorts of lapping, writing, printing, brown, tea and tobacco papers of his own manufacture'[27] and cautioned against employing James Reid who had run away from the manufactory before the end of his contract.[28] The machinery of the paper mill was finally put up for sale in 1805.[29] This included one engine and two vats; evidently considerable downsizing had taken place since 1777. The site was taken over by Robert Gemmell and developed for cotton manufacture.

After Wolfenden's Lambeg mill, the next known paper mill was the one set up by William Ash near Magherafelt, in Tullylinkisay townland, Co. Londonderry, in about 1725. Ash was of a well-connected family, with lands, forges and ironworks, the inheritance of which was assigned to him to exclude a dissolute older brother. After travels to London and Dublin with his father, he set up the paper mill near home; and then took up a career in the militia.[30] Soon after, he acquired a considerable estate from his mother's side and added her name Rainey to his own. William Ash Rainey was decribed as, 'an innocent weak man who let off his estate at extremely low rates, throwing away his prosperity though ignorance', and he became very poor.[31] Little more is known of the paper mill – it did not merit a mention in a rental of 1752.[32] The existence of a paper-maker of Tullylinkisay in 1759 and 1768, Thomas Wallace, is known from his witnessing a deed for Francis Joy.[33] The *Ordnance Survey Memoirs* fairsheets of 1836 noted, 'the ruin of an old paper mill ... lately occupied by the late Thomas Wallace, but ceased to manufacture paper about 1776 in consequence of the water being insufficient.'[34] Connections between the Rainey and the Joy families,[35] and residence of his wife's sister in Magherafelt,[36] might have led Francis Joy to his first glimpse of a paper mill.

That Francis Joy was able to acquire four existing paper mills in 1739–40 indicates that paper-making had become established in a small way by the 1730s if not before. One paper mill at Ballymena was in the hands of John Pettycrew,[37] a name of French origin which suggests also the origin of his trade skills. A Ballymena deed of 1741 refers to paper-maker William Pettycrew,[38] and other deeds refer to another, Stephen Halgan,[39] whose old paper mill at Ballymena Joy leased out as a flax mill in 1750.[40] The establishment of these mills probably owed to the cutting of a mill race from the River Braid some years earlier by the landlord Sir Robert Adair, to encourage industry to his estates.[41]

The two paper mills in Ballygrooby townland adjacent to Randalstown were occupied in 1740 by Daniel Shakershaft, James Wolfenden, Jacob Wolfenden, Robert Russell, John Tedford and James Cambell.[42] The Wolfenden family had thus extended paper-making to other parts of the north of Ireland. Russell and Cambell were probably descended from the Scottish emigrants who arrived in the area between 1680 and 1695 at the encouragement of the estate owner Rose O'Neill (afterwards Marchioness of Antrim) of Shane's Castle in Randalstown. She was credited also with the establishment of manufactories for improving the prosperity of her tenantry.[43]

FRANCIS JOY

The story of Francis Joy is generally well-known but merits a reminder. He was from an affluent farming family in Co. Antrim and settled in Belfast as a conveyancer and public-notary. He acquired further property and connections through his first wife, Margaret Martin, granddaughter of a Sovereign of Belfast. Due to a bad debt, he found himself the owner of a printing press and in 1737 founded the *Belfast News Letter*.[44] He was also well-connected through his mother, Jane Ellis of Carrickfergus.[45] In 1739, due to difficulties in the supply of paper from France for their businesses, Joy and two other Belfast printers, James Magee and Samuel Wilson, took over a paper mill in Ballymena. They authorised John Pettycrew to buy rags at the mill and advertised for more paper-makers.[46] James Magee's and Samuel Wilson's names were inserted alongside Joy's in the lease of the Ballymena paper mill for only five years, from 1741;[47] their partnership ended in 1744.[48] Joy's 1750 leases for the two mills in Ballymena were in his sole name,[49] the second being Halgan's old mill, noted above. Joy continued to advertise his Ballymena-made paper until at least 1757.[50] He leased out both mills in 1760.[51]

In 1740 Joy, with Magee and Wilson, took over the two paper mills in Ballygrooby. The following year, 1741, the three printers made over the paper mills to (presumably) young relatives, Thomas Magee, Andrew Wilson and Henry Joy who was about to come of age. Joy's heirs were to take a half share. Francis Joy was to be reimbursed out of the profits above the running costs, and payments were made to the other two printers.[52] It would seem that this arrangement was short-lived and that Francis Joy's personal interest in paper-making increased. In 1742, he mortgaged the Ballygrooby mills to raise £200[53] and in 1743 began the developments in Randalstown cited in his parliamentary petitions. He moved to Randalstown about the time of his second marriage in 1745,[54] leaving the Belfast newspaper and printing business to be run by his sons Henry and Robert.

In his petition for aid to parliament in 1747,[55] Francis Joy outlined the efforts, achievements and expenditure of the previous four years. He had erected two paper engines (Hollander machines) at Randalstown and another in Ballymena in 1747 which cost £600 – most of his wealth. At two mills he made writing and printing papers and brown paper at the other (at Randalstown, engine installed 1746[56]). He had made great efforts to increase the rag supply, with the successful result that other paper mills in his part of the Kingdom could also be supplied. In his first year of trial he made more writing paper than any mill outside Dublin but due to lack of skilled workmen and clean water (unpolluted by flax-steeping) he had had to give up. He had lately discovered a method of making good quality paper from refuse of the flax industry and sought assistance for the setting up of a new mill in the best Dutch manner with a clean water supply. With such he could bring in skilled foreign workmen and be able to promote the industry in the north of Ireland – using the raw materials and water supplies available for home manufacture and possibly export. The petition was well received initially but no funding resulted. Francis Joy submitted a second petition in 1749.[57] He outlined his contributions to local printing and publishing, and to improved bleaching of linen which could be applied to the refuse used for paper-making. He had promoted proper paper-making methods through which four paper engines had been erected in Counties Antrim and Londonderry; other makers had been consulting him. Now he was finding cheap imports of French and Dutch paper a great threat to his enterprise, and bringing clean water to his mills was a particular expense. Parliament awarded him £200.

Francis Joy's frequent advertisements in the *Belfast News Letter* show the products of his three mills covering a wide range of papers:

> Francis Joy makes and sells in Ballymena and Randalstown, variety of good writing paper, and printing paper, and white and blue paper for lapping linen cloth, and also several kinds of brown papers.[58]
>
> These papers are equal in goodness to foreign, and offered to sale cheaper than the like can be imported from abroad. And as the real value of the writing paper, of which there are several sorts, will recommend them upon trial, and has done so to all that have used them (particularly the schools) being smooth and bearing well; it is not doubted but the dealers in paper will give encouragement to the manufacture of their country in preference to France or Holland.[59]
>
> ... inside fine white and bright blue and outside papers for lapping linen cloth, and brown papers of all kinds and as cheap as any made in the kingdom.[60]

A piece of Francis Joy's own watermarked white writing paper survives in his correspondence.[61] Although the first issue of the *News Letter* to carry the phrase '(on paper of his own manufacturing)' was dated 10 June 1746,[62] it hardly means that Joy's own paper was not used until then. Francis Joy was particularly energetic in his rag-collecting schemes.

> He ... is now attempting to procure rags, ropes and the waste of heckled tow at Ballymoney, Coleraine, Derry and Strabane, and places contiguous: He therefore humbly requests that all kinds of linen rags, especially fine may be preserved. If a sufficiency be got to load returning cars or carts he proposes to furnish and send to gentlemen in those parts, such papers as from time to time may be wanted at moderate prices, and hopes to be encouraged by lovers of their country in what is humbly attempted, proposed and requested by Francis Joy.[63]

Of the several mills along the east bank of the River Maine between the cornmills at the bridge at Randalstown itself, and the weir about 1km to the north, a number were in Francis Joy's hands.[64] It has not proved possible so far to identify the precise sites of the mills with certainty. Besides the paper mills, Francis Joy, active also as a linen draper, had a flax mill[65] and a bleaching mill and green[66] which he let and which appears to have been the paper mill once occupied by James Wolfenden and Daniel Shakeshaft.[67] He also had a tuck mill.[68] There was another paper mill operator in Ballygrooby about 1757, John O'Connor the tenant at O'Neill's paper mill,[69] and possibly others.[70] In 1774, Francis Joy advertised for let the mill that he built for paper-making, which adjoined the cornmills in Randalstown, as he was intending to concentrate his paper-making at one mill – he was by then seventy-six years old.[71] However, a deed of 1780 shows Joy still in the possession of two paper mills in Ballygrooby. By 1778 he had been joined in paper-making by William Jackson[72] who married his daughter Frances. Francis Joy continued paper-making until his death in 1790 aged almost ninety-three. William Jackson continued the paper-making business after Francis Joy's death,[73] probably in partnership with his wife. Mrs Jackson's name appears alone in a 1794 advertisement cautioning against a runaway apprentice from Randalstown paper mill.[74] The mill continued in operation until 1815 when Mrs Jackson put it up for sale or let.[75]

JAMES BLOW AND DANIEL BLOW

The Blow family were a dynasty of printers, paper-makers, booksellers and stationers. James Blow (1676–1759) with his brother-in-law Patrick Neill came from Scotland and started Belfast's first printing business in 1694. Neill died in 1705 and Blow became established as Belfast's foremost stationer, printer and publisher, issuing mostly theological works.[76] His daughter Jane married George Grierson, the first of a dynasty of King's Printers in Dublin.[77] James Blow printed several works including bibles with Grierson and it is assumed that this useful contact led to the consumption of much of his paper output; this has yet to be ascertained through watermark studies. James Blow made the paper for a short-lived newspaper the *Belfast Courant*, 1745–46, published by James Magee.[78] This indicates that James Magee had lost interest in the Ballymena mill, and the Blows were indeed making paper before the establishment of their mill at Dunadry in 1747. Reference to the Blows' Falls Road mill identifying it as a paper mill has been found only in property advertisements of 1777 and 1783,[79] but the lands and mills in this part of Edenderry townland were leased to Daniel Blow in 1754 and had been formerly possessed by James Blow.[80] Daniel Blow let the mill to Nathaniel Wilson in the 1780s for a cotton mill.[81]

Daniel Blow (1718–1810) entered into partnership with his father James in 1747,[82] the year that he built the paper mill at Dunadry, and is described as 'printer, bookseller and paper-maker' on the lease.[83] Dubourdieu records that one of the earliest engines (from Scotland and erected by Scotsman, William Bell) was brought in by James and Daniel Blow for their mill near Belfast.[84] In 1750 Daniel Blow received one of the awards, worth £20, from the Dublin Society in the category of building 'the compleatest Mills for making White Paper'.[85] Daniel Blow was also active as a linen draper. His obituary credited him with having improved linen manufacture by introducing the use of acid of vitriol as a sour for bleaching,[86] and there are references to him in the guise of a linen draper in the 1740s[87] and 1750s[88] He leased a flax mill and bleaching mill in Clouney in 1754,[89] and was in partnership with Charles Cunningham, exporting linen to America and trading in imported flaxseed and flax.[90]

In 1759, at the age of about forty-one Daniel Blow inherited the family printing, publishing and bookselling business.[91] It might be surmised that he became less active in linen as he became very productive in printing from that time, besides paper-making.[92] He had married in 1746 and had six children, the youngest being James Blow born 1760,[93] who went into the paper-making side of the business. The oldest son Daniel took on the printing side. From 1780 onwards, Daniel Blow senior identified himself as 'paper-maker' in advertisements for lottery tickets at his shop.[94] Bills sent to the proprietors of the *Northern Star* in 1793 were received from Daniel Blow senior for paper (not for the publication itself) and Daniel Blow junior for printing.[95] The last Daniel Blow imprint appeared in 1794[96] – as the senior approached the age of seventy-six, he was probably considering some retirement. Joshua Gilpin, an American paper-maker touring Europe, called on Daniel Blow in September 1796 and found the 'Old man, 77, very hearty.' 'Has found he has made large fortune.' 'Formerly in printing business but not now'.[97] The son Daniel predeceased the father who made provision for the widow and children in his will of 1810.[98] By 1800, James Blow (1760–1752) was the licensed paper-maker at Dunadry.[99] In 1802 he formed a partnership with John Ward and

Robert Greenfield under the name of Blow, Ward & Co., formally taking over the paper mill at Dunadry.[100]

Joy had stated in his 1749 petition to parliament that four paper engines had been erected in Counties Antrim and Londonderry, and that other makers had been consulting him. Where would these have been? Strictly speaking Wolfenden's mill at Lambeg was in Co. Down, but only on the other side of the river from Co. Antrim. There was Daniel Blow's paper mill at Dunadry; the Blows' Falls Road paper mill was probably operating at this time. In Co. Londonderry there was the mill at Tullylinkisay, but was its water supply worth the investment of a Hollander machine? Evidence has been found only for these mills, Joy's own mills and perhaps another in Randalstown – but it seems there might have been a few others. Dublin Society notices in the *News Letter* in the early 1750s announcing the distribution of premiums to rag gatherers referred to 'the paper-makers near Belfast'.[101] During the second half of the eighteenth century at least nine further paper mills were set up. These included: Finnard (near Rathfriland, Co.Down) by 1767, Cromac (at Belfast) in 1767, Millfield (near Claudy, Co. Londonderry) by 1773, and at Antrim in 1776. The mills at Ballyclare began in 1792 and at Tolands (in Co. Londonderry near Coleraine) in 1794. Other mills of unknown start date, but probably close to the end of the century, were: one in or near Armagh, at Jonesborough (near Newry) and at Ballymagorry (near Strabane). Cromac and Ballyclare paper mills being of particular interest will be described first – Cromac for being the paper mill of Henry and Robert Joy and Ballyclare for its initial association with the *Northern Star*.

CROMAC PAPER MILL, BELFAST

Cromac Mill, a meadowland stroll from Belfast town, was built in 1767–8 by the sons of Francis Joy, Henry Joy (1720–1789) and Robert Joy (1722–1785). As noted above, Francis had tried to interest the young Henry in the Randalstown mills in 1741, but by the mid-1740s it was Francis who had moved away and left his sons to manage the daily business of printing, publishing and bookselling, and producing the *Belfast News Letter*. Francis Joy's advertisements continued to appear in the paper frequently and in prime position: appeals for rags and papers for sale, as well as for a variety of Randalstown community matters. Henry and Robert sold their father's paper alongside imported writing papers, and also received rags for him.

Belfast began to prosper increasingly from the mid-eighteenth century, as economic conditions strengthened in the linen industry and trading, and improved tenure of property encouraged development. In June 1767, the absentee owner of Belfast, the Earl of Donegall arrived in the town to grant and renew leases. Henry Joy acquired rebuilding and repairing leases for their High Street premises, including the printing house,[102] and Robert Joy obtained the same for properties in Bridge St. and Carrickfergus Street.[103] Henry Joy acquired the lease from May 1767 for the immediate site of the paper mill, an area of 1*a* 2*r* 30*p*, situated on the south side of Cromack Dock or River, a little to the west of the wooden bridge in the Demesne of Belfast.[104] It would appear that little time was lost in building. 'Joy's Mill' was located on 'A plan of the River Lagon, and the intended navigable canal from Belfast to Loughneagh', surveyed in 1768, which was printed by the Joys.[105]

By April 1769, Francis Joy had cause to complain mildly that he, 'being lately deprived of getting rags in Belfast (from whence had been mostly supplied)' had to try and procure them from somewhere else.[106] In the summer of 1769 advertisements were placed for '2 or 3 poor women of good character for picking linen rags for which more will be given than they can earn at the wheel,'[107] and for 'an apprentice to the paper-making business now carrying on at Cromack near Belfast.'[108] In October 1769, they advertised 'a few reams of very fine blue paper just made at Cromack paper mill … for hanging rooms …'.[109] Leases for more lands were taken out from May 1769: for a small extension to the paper mill site, land for eight workmen's houses near the Saltwater Bridge, and between them, for the Town Parks to the south of the Blackstaff River.[110] The mill and houses appear on a 1770 Donegall estate map.[111]

Throughout the 1770s, Henry and Robert Joy used the columns of the *News Letter* for advertising the papers laid in from their mill at Cromack, alongside imported papers and a variety of stationery goods. The serious matter of rag supplies was broached in the editorial:

> As Irish manufacture is likely to be preferred in every branch the patriotic ladies of this kingdom as well as the school mistresses, milliners, plain-workers &c. are particularly requested to imitate the first personages in Great Britain, and place bags in some convenient part of their houses, for the saving of linen rags, so very essential to promote our manufacture. The neglect of this domestic economy in the better sort of people is the cause why Irish paper is not equal to foreign, as the collecting or saving rags in this kingdom, is not thought an object worth attending to by any but the poor, whose habitations being smokey and linen chiefly handlecloth render the produce of their industry unfit for any but the coarsest paper. We therefore hope to see proper attention paid to this branch of economy which will not only serve as a handsome perquisite to the servants, but also afford this kingdom as good paper as any made in England or Holland, and save the considerable sums sent out of this impoverished kingdom for that article.[112]

It appears that power for the wheel, supplied by the tide flowing to the Lagan down Cromack Dock from the Blackstaff River including its original outlet to the Lagan contained by the Long Bank, was considered in need of improvement. In 1780, Henry Joy took a lease of *7a 2r* of land to the north of the paper mill, containing the original outlet of the Blackstaff to the Lagan,[113] and created an efficient mill dam; it soon became known as Joy's Dam. During the 1780s, Henry Joy took other leases including those for lands at New Enclosure in Belfast, Cromack Woods and Lower and Upper Malone and a building lease in Linenhall Street – indicating that business was profitable.[114]

In addition to editing and producing the *Belfast News Letter*, the printing and stationer's business in all its other aspects, the notary office, and later the paper mill, Henry and Robert Joy developed significant other interests. From 1752 onwards, they were much involved with the Belfast Charitable Society which was set up to build a poorhouse, hospital and a new church. Their names appear in decades of Committee Minute Books in pursuit of tasks both mundane and employing their professional skills, and their watermark appeared in three Committee books of the late 1770s.[115] The Joy brothers were instrumental in the administration of fund-raising lotteries, acting as secretaries, producing and issuing tickets and advertising, as well as chasing up debtors. In 1770, a reported forgery of a lottery ticket led Robert Joy to get a mould made for watermarked paper for future issues of tickets. After protracted consideration of professional alternatives, it was Robert Joy's plan upon which the Poorhouse was eventually built, completed in 1774.[116] Running the Poorhouse continued to occupy the Joys, particularly Robert. What started off as an enterprising idea to employ the industrious youth, developed by the early 1780s into the fully established cotton manufacture business of Joys, McCabe & McCracken. From this beginning, the manufacture of cotton sprang up around Belfast generally and it had become a major industry by the turn of that century. Thus cotton and charitable works perhaps rather took Robert Joy's focus away from his printing and paper interests.

Henry and Robert Joy were highly esteemed for their enterprise, integrity and compassion. They worked the family business so closely together that it was not possible to distinguish who actually owned what. What would happen in terms of inheritance did matter to Robert's son Henry Joy jun. (1754–1835) who appears to have discussed it at length with his close friend Michael Bruce – revealed in the latter's correspondence of 1778. Bruce referred to:

> the evident and absolute necessity of making a thorough reformation and an entire new settlement of the property and profits of your father's and uncle's business ... to put an end at once to the numberless disputes and quarrels which would otherwise arise from the shameful irregularity that has reigned such a number of years in the house … you made some objections as to the difficulty of dividing and settling the freeholds … [117]

The paper mill was singled out as a valuable part of the trade. Bruce made some practical suggestions and urged his friend to set about the task. In an affectionate letter that Michael Bruce wrote as his last to his friend before taking ship for the United States, he offered two pieces of advice: firstly to settle the family business affairs and secondly not to marry until he had the means to support a wife and family in comfort, and had seen something of the world first. Bruce sailed, and was lost at sea.[118] Henry Joy jun. took heed and went on a tour of England the following summer, 1779. He made notes on art, architecture, manufactures, geology and scenery, and described the speakers at a debate in the

House of Commons. He visited the famous Mr Whatman's Turkey Paper Mill in Maidstone in Kent and made detailed technical observations that reveal a real interest in and knowledge of paper-making. This was between visits to the military camps at Cocksheath and Chatham.[119]

Of the five sons of Henry and Robert Joy, it was Robert's son Henry Joy jun. who took to the printing and paper business. He became editor of the *News Letter* in 1782 when he was taken into the partnership, the business becoming 'H & R Joy & Co.'[120] It was politics that enthused the young Henry Joy jun. who was a leading member of the Volunteer movement. Empowered by the independent-thinking Presbyterian middle class of Belfast, the movement soon turned its attention from military matters to pressing forward radical ideals. As a pamphlet printer and editor of the influential *News Letter*, Joy had a central role in promoting the movement's political aims of free trade and constitutional reform. Moderately radical politics were good for business, appealing to a wide section of the newspaper-buying public. In the 1790s, radical opinion branched towards the more actively revolutionary with the founding of Societies of United Irishmen, and in Belfast a rival newspaper, the *Northern Star*. The contest between the *News Letter* and *Northern Star* and Henry Joy's motives for selling out in 1795 have been closely examined;[121] mainly he doubted the economic viability of a newspaper of his political stance.

The wills and deaths of Robert and Henry Joy, in 1785 and 1789 respectively, left Henry Joy jun. with half ownership of the family printing and paper business and the other half with the three sons and son-in-law of Henry Joy sen.[122] Martha McTier, whose letters commented on decades of Belfast's political and social scene, wrote in December 1792 that Joy was having a sore time in a dispute with all his relatives about the profit he was making on the newspaper.[123] Perhaps Michael Bruce's warnings were coming true. In 1793, Williamson was commissioned to survey the properties of the Messrs Joy. First advertised, in November 1794, was the copyright of the *Belfast News Letter* to be sold by contract, preparatory to a general sale of various partnership properties.[124] The *News Letter* of 19–23 January 1795 carried an exhaustive advertisement for sale of joint properties of

Henry Joy and the devisees in trust of the late Henry Joy deceased, to be auctioned on 24th March. These included the properties in High Street, Change Alley and Carrickfergus Street; the concerns at Cromack, and Cromack Wood and Town Parks adjoining. The premises at Cromack included the large paper mill, supplied with a stream of pure spring water; two roads communicating with the town, one by Saltwater Bridge, the other by the new Shambles; four houses for workmen, a stable for four horses, a large hayloft, coach house and a cow house. The contents of the paper mill were listed as: two vats, engines, wet and dry presses, stuff chests, boiler, pressing and lay boards, blocks, planks, wire washers, trebles and lines. Included with the lot was also the *7a 2r* chiefly covered by that extensive sheet of water on the north side of the Mall embacked for increasing the quantity for the water wheel, and eight houses for workmen and some rear gardens on the Malone Road at the Saltwater Bridge. Possession was to be given with the right of the present proprietors to finish whatever paper had been made and unfinished at the time of the sale. In order that the purchaser of the concern should have every encouragement, all the materials, implements and everything else used in the manufacture was to be sold at a valuation to be determined by the opinion of two indifferent persons. The land in Cromack Wood was under reservation to the purchaser, it containing the source of spring water for the mill. While the *News Letter* was sold to a firm from Edinburgh, George Joy, Henry Joy of Dublin, James Joy and David Tomb assigned their interests in the Cromack paper mill and mill dam properties to Henry Joy for £1,200 5s.[125] In his last issues of the *News Letter* in May 1795, Henry Joy announced from Cromack paper mill, 'that the business of that mill is henceforth to be carried on in the most extensive manner, on his own account; and that the place of sale will, in a few days, be removed from the usual one in the front street to the Warehouse in rear. Future orders for paper are to be addressed to himself.'[126]

Joshua Gilpin visited the mill of 'Jay [sic] & Co.' in September 1796. He found it,

> very much on plan of ours in America. The vatts on each side of the engine, and three stories high. ... single engine on old plan. No floor

> in the vatt room or engine house. Mill in every respect but indifferent. Makes some tolerable paper but not equal to our best in America. ... have rag room over the engine. Rag store over the loft. Some English screws. Some made here, prefer the first.[127]

Joy advertised, 'a large assortment of papers of various kinds, for the use of schools, also fine propatria and post, tea papers, large and small brown, and tobacco papers; very fine blue and white papers for linen drapers; besides several other denominations.' He added that, 'Exporting merchants and grocers will find their interest in giving a preference to this home manufacture, and the quality of the several papers is good and never varies'. Orders for stationery of the finest British and Irish paper were invited.[128] By 1806, a second engine had been purchased[129] indicating an expansion of business. In 1810, Joy leased the Cromac mill to the firm of Blow, Ward & Co. which had been working the mill at Dunadry since 1802.[130]

BALLYCLARE PAPER MILL, CO. ANTRIM

At the turn of the year 1793, a new paper manufactory was announced in the *Belfast News Letter*: 'Arthur Darley & Co. have for sale at their shop in High Street, two, four, six and eight pound paper, tea paper and tobacco paper of the manufacture of their mill at Ballyclare. They will in a few months have ready a variety of writing and printing paper, with inside, outside and seven-eight lapping for linens ...'[131] Arthur Darley was a public notary who trained under Henry Joy: in 1788 he was at the office of Messrs Joy in Belfast[132] and was a witness to Henry Joy's will.[133] In 1789 and 1790 he gained his legal qualifications and appointments.[134] In February 1791, Arthur Darley started looking for a mill and a mortgage[135] and found the premises he had been looking for in a flour mill, with a dwelling house and garden, lying on the Six Mile Water in the townland of Ballyclare in the Parish of Ballynure. This was granted to him and his partners James Jackson, a surgeon of Newtownards, and James Kenley.[136] Both Darley and Jackson became involved with the *Northern Star*. In January 1792 Samuel Nielson was to prevail upon one Mr A. Darley to act as an agent in preparations for the distribution of the newspaper;[137] presumably Darley had gained knowledge of newspaper distribution at the offices of Messrs Joy. By the end of 1792, Darley was advertising his continuing services as a public notary from his own office in Belfast.[138]

An examination of the watermarks in extant sets of the *Northern Star*[139] gives a clear indication of the source of the paper it was printed on. From the start in January 1792 to mid-March 1793, the paper was usually watermarked 'M' and occasionally 'DMD' with 'DMD' more common at the end of that time. 'DMD' has been identified with the watermark of Darby McDonnell, one of the famous family of Dublin paper-makers.[140] The *Northern Star* received an account for news paper directly from Darby McDonnell in March 1793.[141] The rather unspecific 'M' watermark has not been identified, but might well come from an unspecified McDonnell family mould. From August 1792 (and probably before) to July 1793, William Gilbert acted as the news paper supply agent, getting it duty stamped in Dublin before sending it to Belfast.[142] William Gilbert was a bookbinder, bookseller and auctioneer of Dublin, and a United Irishman, with family connections with William Magee and Robert Callwell who were both proprietors of the *Northern Star*.[143] By May 1793, he was pressing for some realisable and regular payment for the stamped paper he had supplied. *Northern Stars* between April and early October 1793 were then largely without discernable watermarks with occasional exceptions – indicating difficulties with finding another regular supply cheaply. Between May and mid July 1793 every half dozen issues or so, one with a 'JOY' watermark, appeared. The watermark 'AD & Co' of Arthur Darley & Co. appeared for the first time in early June 1793 and the paper was used regularly through October and November 1793. That batch had not been duty stamped, a fact declared in the publication with a view to paying later[144] with the exact deficit sworn by the affidavit of an employee.[145] Recourse was then made to Joy's and unwatermarked paper, followed by further regular supplies from Arthur Darley & Co. from February to mid April 1794 when again Joy's paper had to be used for three publications. A note of 17 April 1794 reads, 'S Neilson's compliments to Mr Joy, has some apprehensions that he may be so disappointed in paper as to be straightened for two or three publications say 12–15 reams, would be glad to know if Mr Joy could let me have that quantity next week in case it should be wanted'.[146]

In November 1794 James and Andrew Jackson announced,

> that they continue the manufactory of paper at Ballyclare Mill on their own account, where they have ready for sale a considerable quantity of the different kinds, the quality and prices of which on trial they hope will give general satisfaction. NB In a few days they will deliver a parcel of each sort at the Star Office where their friends in future may depend on being regularly supplied.[147]

As noted above, James Jackson had been in partnership with Arthur Darley. By 1795 he was acting in a secretarial capacity for the proprietors of the *Northern Star*, his signature adorning many of the promissory notes of payment to the proprietors.[148] Promissory notes to Andrew Jackson for paper were signed by another agent of the proprietors, Matthew Smith.[149] Some 'AD & Co' watermarks appeared in December 1794 and early 1795, the wire motifs on the mill's moulds not yet replaced. From March 1795 the 'JJ' and 'JJ&Co' watermarks of James Jackson & Co. appeared and continued to the end of the *Northern Star*'s existence in April 1797. The irregularities in news paper supply to the *Northern Star* appear to reflect both the financial pressures that beset the proprietors and some practical difficulties experienced by their agents at the Ballyclare paper mill. As well as the *Northern Star*, other radical publications were issued from the *Northern Star* press. One was the first magazine in Irish, *Bolg an tSolair:* or, *Gaelic Magazine*. Examination of the Ulster Museum's copy shows it to have been printed on paper from a pair of moulds with the 'A D & Co' watermarks in rather worn condition: from one the 'D' is missing and from the other part of the 'D' is missing – leaving it reading 'A I & Co' which might have suited Andrew Jackson.[150]

In March 1798, James Jackson and Andrew Jackson sold the lease of the Ballyclare paper mill to Robert Simms and William Simms, and Matthew Smith for £1500.[151] The new proprietors announced that they intended 'carrying on the paper business there in the most extensive manner, under the firm of Simms & Smith.'[152] Matthew Smith had worked in the office of the *Northern Star* for a number of years, and the Simms brothers had been two of the twelve proprietors. They were known as tanners and energetic merchants in business circles, and for their activities as United Irishmen. They acquired the paper mill just months before becoming embroiled in the 1798 Rebellion. For his part in this, Robert Simms was imprisoned in Scotland from 1799 to 1802. In 1800, the licensed paper-maker at Ballyclare was one James Smith.[153] In 1806 Simms and Smith tried to sell the Ballyclare mill,[154] apparently without success, but by 1809 it was in the hands of Simms & McIntyre.[155] This was David Simms, a former compositor at the *Northern Star* who had begun a printing business in 1797 with the remains salvaged from its destroyed offices, and George McIntyre, a printer from the house of Warrin. They had set up a partnership in the business of printing, bookselling and stationery in December 1806.[156] The Ballyclare mill was advertised for sale in late 1815[157] and taken over by the firm of Blow, Ward and Co., their third mill in addition to Dunadry and Cromac.[158] Simms & McIntyre continued as paper merchants and in printing, bookselling and stationery, and were to publish series of cheap paperbacks by which their business came to flourish.[159] Henry Joy provided an interesting comment on the relative fortunes of the paper mill proprietors of Belfast, and others, at the end of the eighteenth century. At a meeting of the applotment assessment for the town of Belfast, spring 1799, he made a list of estimated worth of the businessmen, which included: Henry Joy, paper-maker, £12,000; Robert Simms, tanner, £7000; William Simms, tanner, £7000; William Magee, printer £13,000; and Daniel Blow, paper-maker, £6,000.[160]

FINNARD PAPER MILL, CO. DOWN

The earliest reference found so far to the paper mill at Finnard is a sale advertisement of 1767: '… the one third part of a paper mill with all utensils in compleat order, situated in the townland of Finards, four miles distant from Newry. Proposals will be received by Mr Robert Rainey in Boat Street Newry; plenty of rags to be had at said place.'[161] This Robert Rainey appears to have been a third cousin of William Ash Rainey who established the paper mill near Magherafelt.[162] Newry's importance as a port was rising rapidly with the building of a ship canal between 1759 and 1769, augmenting the Newry Navigation between Lough Neagh and Newry completed in 1742. There was evidently a good market for paper around Newry at this time. James Daniel, who had just built a large paper mill at Newbridge, Co. Kildare,[163] opened a warehouse in Newry for his own papers and for receiving rags,[164] and George Stevenson, printer and bookseller, advertised extensive stocks of paper.[165] 'The town and lands of Finnards called Papervale, the paper mill, machinery and utensils … and houses thereto' were released to Henry Thetford, or Tedford, in 1784.[166] In 1791, he advertised for either, 'an active discreet partner' or to, 'sell out his interest in a lease of a mill in compleat order, with all the machinery, having lately undergone a thorough repair.'[167] One John Tedford had been an occupier with members of the Wolfenden family of the paper mills in Ballygrooby prior to Francis Joy's takeover in 1740. The Tedford family remained in paper-making at Finnard until the early 1830s, when they fell foul of the Excise.

MILLFIELD PAPER MILL NEAR CLAUDY, CO. LONDONDERRY

The earliest reference so far found to the paper mill near Claudy in Co. Londonderry is an advertisement in the *Londonderry Journal* in 1773, an appeal for rags for Mr McClintock's paper mill – showing the procurement of the raw materials as an overriding concern. To save the rag collectors around Manor Cunningham, Letterkenny, Rathmelton and Raphoe from the inconvenience of the ferry, rags would be purchased from them at Castle Cunningham. Any kind or size of paper that could not be obtained from Douglas & Blyth, the printers in Derry, could be ordered from the mill through the printers.[168] The mill was up for let in 1779, the advertisement noting the proximity of nearby towns, Derry, Strabane, Newtown Stewart and Newtown Limavady, all considerable cloth markets within sixteen miles.[169] The paper mill was leased to William Mathews and Robert McMurdy in 1793.[170] The Mathews family worked the mill until the late 1830s, becoming notorious for crimes against the Excise.

ANTRIM PAPER MILL

The paper mill in Antrim, according to Lewis, was founded in 1776 but burnt down a few years later and was then rebuilt[171] in 1783.[172] It appears to have been then operated by the Johnstone family (however, between about 1815 and 1830, they were associated with the Boghead paper mill which was about a mile from Antrim, so there is room for uncertainty). One Michael Johnstone had been an apprentice to Francis Joy in 1741.[173] In 1790, the partnership between John, James and Thomas Johnson was dissolved and the defendants' property including a large quantity of brown and whited brown paper, machinery of a paper mill, and tenement in Antrim were auctioned by the order of court to pay off debts to the plaintiff Hugh Swan,[174] who was a bleacher in the Muckamore area upstream of Antrim and Boghead. There was a further sale of paper and rags at Antrim paper mill in 1792.[175] By 1800 the licensed paper manufacturer at Antrim was Alex. Ledlie & Co.;[176] Ledlie had been in partnership with Hugh Swan.[177] Ledlie was involved in various businesses and evolving partnerships that can be traced through newspaper advertisements from 1785, when he was in linen manufacture, through the 1790s and 1800s as he and long-term business associates Hugh Montgomery and James Ferguson (of the linen merchant family) accrued the corn and flour and paper mills, and brewery in Antrim.[178] The paper mill at Antrim was to become one of the largest in the north of Ireland in the nineteenth century.

OTHER LATE EIGHTEENTH CENTURY PAPER MILLS

The four mills remaining to be noted all appear to have been set up in the last few years of the eighteenth century and there are very few details of their earliest existence. They might be better seen in the context of the beginning of the increase in the number of small paper mills that occurred during the early decades of the nineteenth century, beyond the scope of this discussion. The paper mill in Tullans townland, parish of Coleraine, Co. Londonderry was erected in 1794, at a cost of £2000, by the first proprietor Robert Church who occupied it to 1804. He was succeeded by members of the Eccles family[179] of

Ballyrashane. According to Eccles family information, one William Eccles had been manager at Dunadry in the 1740s. James Eccles had come to Tullans in 1794; he was the son of Samuel Eccles of Antrim who started paper mills at Moylena[180] (near Antrim). The Roan paper mill in Roughan townland, parish of Derrynoose, a few miles south of Armagh, was occupied by the Girvin family of linen drapers who had been established in the area on the River Callen for at least several decades.[181] The mill known as Ballymagorry in MacCrackens townland in the parish of Leckpatrick, Co. Tyrone was in the hands of George Lyon.[182] There was also a mill at Jonesborough, Co.Armagh.[183]

PAPER MILLS AT THE END OF THE EIGHTEENTH CENTURY FROM THE EVIDENCE OF THE EXCISE

Paper excise was introduced to Ireland in 1798 (paper-making had been taxed in Great Britain since 1712) and excise statistics show the number of paper mills and some indication of their relative size and type at the end of the eighteenth century. An early statistical table provides, 'A view of the Paper Duties in Ireland in the year ending 25 December 1799 and year to 25 March 1803'.[184] The individual mills are not listed for these statistics, but the excise districts are and as there were only a few mills, the figures can be interpreted by comparing them to the statistics of 1806, in 'An acount of the produce of paper duty in the Excise Distr. in the years ending 25th March 1806'[185] which lists districts, the paper-makers' names and situations of their mills (see Tables 1 and 2). Also given are the numbers of engines and vats and total duty charged (shown here rounded to whole pounds). The list here (Table 2) is ordered by the size of mill that can be deduced first by number of engines and vats, then by amount of duty paid which was rather dependent on the honesty of the trader and determination of the excise officers.

TABLE 1

To compare excise duties (rounded figures) collected per district from Excise Statistics for 1799, 1803 and 1806

*Lisburn district 1799 and 1803 would have included the Wolfenden's mill which closed in 1805.

DISTRICT	MILLS IN 1806	YEAR ENDING 25 MAR 1799	1803	1806
Armagh	Roan, Armagh	£68	£45	£160
Coleraine	Tolands	£129	£100	£216
Larne	Antrim, Randalstown, Boghead	£450	£327	£635
Lisburn*	Ballyclare, Dunadry, Cromac	£931	£1200	£1331
Londonderry	Millfield	£100	£258	£254
Newry	Finnard, Warrenpoint	£83	£504	£1105
Strabane	Ballymagorry	£187	£212	£192
Dundalk	Jonesborough	£58	£242	£300

TABLE 2

Extracts of excise statistics 1806

* The Ballyclare mill was up for sale in 1806 which might account for its comparative low productivity.

** Identity not certain

PAPER-MAKER	LOCATION	NO. ENGINES	NO. VATS	DUTY PAID YR. TO 25 MARCH 1806	% CLASS PAPER MADE 1ST	2ND	3RD
Henry Joy	Cromac, Belfast	2	2	£610	36	18	46
Thomas Black	Warrenpoint	1	3	£878	34	36	30
Blow Ward & Co.	Dunadry	1	2	£581	13	37	50
Alex. Ledlie	Antrim	1	2	£366	16	40	44
C Walsh	Jonesborough, Newry	1	2	£300	41	25	34
Robert Tedford	Finnard, Rathfriland	1	2	£227	17	8	75
Lyons & McCrae	Ballymagorry, Strabane	1	2	£192	2	14	84
Simms & Smyth	Ballyclare*	1	2	£140	8	24	68
W Matthews	Millfield, near Claudy	1	1	£254		5	95
James Eccles	Tolands, near Coleraine	1	1	£216			100
Arch. Douglas	Randalstown	1	1	£192			100
P Doran	Armagh	1	1	£135			100
R Garvin	Roan, near Armagh	1	1	£83			100
J Patterson	Antrim(Boghead/Moylinny)**	1	1	£77			100

The excise classes and rates of duty chargeable on paper in Ireland at this time (year ending 25th March 1806) were 'first class paper' ('writing and drawing') at 3d per lb, 'second class paper' ('coloured or whited brown') at 2d per lb, and 'third class paper' ('brown' paper made from old ropes and cordage) at 1d per lb.[186] Printing paper was in the first class while the range of wrapping paper, including lapping paper used by linen drapers, was covered by the other two classes. Given the widespread tendency in Ireland to cheat the Excise, it might be supposed that a little common printing and wrapping paper (other than brown) was made surreptitiously at mills declaring only 'third class' paper – as would have been before the tax was imposed.

It has been shown that the earliest paper mills in the north of Ireland, begun in the first quarter of the eighteenth century, were situated in the localities where their Protestant immigrant proprietors were already established with textile concerns: Crommelin's mill at Lisburn and the Wolfendens' mills at Lambeg. The local gentry founder of the early mill at Tullylinkisay had unrelated interests and the site proved to be a poor choice for water. While the precise origins of the Ballymena and Randalstown paper mills are unknown, all were first occupied by those of continental Protestant or Scottish immigrant descent in areas where industrial development had been earlier encouraged by the landlords. The 1740s saw Francis Joy and Daniel Blow actively advancing the paper industry through technological improvement and the establishment of half a dozen paper mills between them. But then only four further paper mills were set up prior to the flurry of them that appeared as the century reached its end. It would seem that practical opportunity was limited for taking advantage of the increased need for linen lapping, goods wrapping and printing paper that undoubtedly accompanied the expansion of the linen industry and trade. The relationship between the paper and linen industries merits further detailed examination.

A pattern of the paper industry – in the size, location and type of paper mills – emerged by the end of eighteenth century, albeit from a very small number of establishments compared to the staples of industry in the region. The largest paper mills produced all classes of paper. They were situated close to the main trading and most populous areas and required a supply of clean water and water power. These included the mill at Cromac in Belfast and those at Ballyclare, Dunadry and Antrim situated on the Six Mile Water (where there were also other water-powered industries).There was a second cluster of mills broadly around Newry, at Warrenpoint, Finnard and Jonesborough, of small size at the very end of the century. However, comparing the 1799 and 1806 excise statistics, these were about to expand, both in terms of increase in production and better class of paper produced. There was also soon to be a second mill in the populous area of Armagh. This area had the advantage of the Newry Navigation and Belfast-Dublin passing trade. The lone paper mills at Tolands, Millfield and Ballymagorry were of moderate size serving west Tyrone and northern Londonderry and Antrim; they made mainly brown wrapping paper for the needs of grocers and clothiers. An 1806 map showing mail coach roads of Ireland might be taken to indicate the best lines of road communications around the end of the eighteenth century,[187] on which nearly all the paper mills were to be found. The main cross route from Belfast to Coleraine was via Dunadry, Antrim and Randalstown, with a bye-branch to Ballyclare. From Coleraine, the route arched around via Londonderry to Strabane. Newry was at the focus of several mail coach routes: Belfast to Dublin which passed through Jonesborough; a cross road to Armagh; a bye-road through Rathfriland which passed directly in front of the Finnard paper mill, and a bye-road from Warrenpoint.

As shown with the Joy and Blow family enterprises, and *Northern Star* production, printing and newspaper publication created a need for paper which was often best answered by taking charge of a local supply. Numbers of printers increased in Belfast during the century, and provincial printing spread to several towns: Newry, Armagh, Downpatrick, Londonderry and Strabane, thus providing some market for common printing paper. As part of the research underlying this article, watermark and paper examination studies are to be undertaken to provide a clearer view of the use of home-produced paper for printing and publication in the north of Ireland.

Thus the eighteenth century saw the foundation of a paper industry in the north of Ireland. The number of paper mills began to increase around the turn of the nineteenth century and in the following decades, as the demand for paper increased. In the new century the paper industry everywhere was to face significant challenges and developments: the search for new raw materials and the invention of the paper-making machine. In Ireland, the newly introduced tax on paper was to impose an intolerable burden on a low level industry, leaving the survivors facing the difficulties of furthering a capital-hungry industry.

ACKNOWLEDGEMENTS

I would like to thank the Ulster Museum, particularly Dr Jim McGreevy, Head of Conservation, for supporting me in my research, and my colleagues Robert Heslip, Trevor Parkhill and Dr Vivienne Pollock in the History Department for their unfailing assistance and encouragement. My thanks are due also to the staff of the Public Record Office of Northern Ireland, the Linen Hall Library and Belfast Central Library for their helpfulness in providing access to the invaluable collections in their care.

NOTES

1 John Dubourdieu, *Statistical survey of the County of Antrim* (2 vols, Dublin,1812), ii, pp. 413–4.

2 C Benson & M Pollard, 'The rags of Ireland are by no means the same: Irish paper used in the *Statutes* at large' in *The Long Room* (Autumn/Winter 1970), pp. 18–25.

3 D.C. Coleman, *The British paper industry 1495–1860* (Oxford, 1958), pp. 3–4.

4 A. H. Shorter, *Paper making in the British Isles: an historical and geographical study* (Newton Abbot, 1971), p. 16.

5 James W. Phillips, *Printing and bookselling in Dublin 1670–1800; a bibliographical enquiry* (Dublin, 1998), pp. 151–155.

6 Ibid., pp. 164–169.

7 *Belfast News Letter*, 4 Dec. 1750, 13 Mar.1753. The *Belfast News Letter* Index 1737–1800, compiled by Dr John C Greene, (www.ucs.louisiana.edu/bnl/-) (Jul.–2002–2 Nov. 2004) has proved invaluable.

8 Dubourdieu, *Statistical survey of Co. Antrim*, ii, pp. 413–4.

9 *Journal of the House of Commons of Ireland* (4th edit., 20 vols, Dublin 1798), ii, appendix clix (Belfast Central Library Newspaper Library microfilm).

10 Brian Mackey, 'Overseeing the foundation of the Irish linen industry: the rise and fall of the Crommelin Legend' in *The European linen industry in historical perspective*, eds. Brenda Collins and Philip Ollerenshaw (Oxford, 2003), pp. 99–122.

11 Samuel Smiles, *The Huguenots: their settlements, churches and industries in England and Ireland* (London, 1880), p. 297.

12 D.C. Coleman, *The British paper industry*, pp. 78–79.

13 Mary Pollard, 'White paper-making in Ireland in the 1690s' in *Proceedings of the Royal Irish Academy*, lxxvii, C (1977), no. 6, pp. 223–234.

14 Dubourdieu, *Statistical survey of Co. Antrim*, ii, pp. 413–4.

15 H. C. Marshall, *The parish of Lambeg* (Lisburn, 1933), p. 39.

16 John Dubourdieu, *Statistical survey of the County of Down* (Dublin, 1802), p. 238.

17 Hugh McCall, *Ireland and her staple manufactures* (Belfast, 1865), p. 25.

18 Dublin, Registry of Deeds, vol 128, p. 11, no. 85742, (PRONI: microfilm).

19 Hertford Estate Rent Rolls, 1719 (PRONI, D/427, vol 1, p. 102: microfilm).

20 Hertford Estate map, 1726 (PRONI, D/427/3B).

21 Registry of Deeds, vol 129, p. 24, no. 86124.

22 *Belfast News Letter*, 27–30 Aug. 1776.

23 Marshall, *The parish of Lambeg*, pp. 37–39: a tombstone in Lambeg church-yard reads, 'here lies the body of the first master papermaker who excelled. Died on 8th Apr. 1774, aged 72 …' William Cassidy jun., *Lambeg*

Churchyard, inscriptions on old tombtones (Belfast, 1937), p. 36: the tombstone in Lambeg churchyard, south side, no.65 reads 'here lieth the body —— / Peter C—— master / papermaker who exceled. /Died the 8th Apr. 1774, aged 62 years'. It is next to no. 66, of the Rev. Saumarez Dubourdieu, who died 14 Dec. 1812, aged 96 years and 3 months.

24 *Belfast News Letter*, 24–27 Feb. 1778.

25 Ibid., 23 May, 20-24 June, 7-10 Oct. 1777.

26 Ibid., 14-18 May 1779.

27 Ibid., 5 Jan. 1802.

28 Ibid., 5 Feb. 1802.

29 *Belfast Commercial Chronicle*, 16 Oct. 1805.

30 Thomas Ash, *The Ash Mss* 1735, ed. Edward J Martin (Dundonald, 1890), p. 19.

31 Henry Joy jun., notes on Rainey connections in the geneology of the Joy family (Belfast, Linen Hall Library, Joy Manuscripts, 6, pp. 372–377).

32 W.H. Maitland, *A history of Magherafelt* (Cookstown, 1916), p. 19: information published in the Salters Company, *The Terrier*, half year to Nov. 1752.

33 Registry of Deeds, vol 254, p. 483, no. 169162.

34 *Ordnance Survey Memoirs of Ireland, parishes of Co. Londonderry I,* (eds) Angelique Day & Patrick McWilliams (Belfast, 1990), vol 6, p. 105.

35 Henry Joy jun., notes on Rainey connections (LHL, Joy MSS, 6, pp. 372–377).

36 *Funerals register of the First Presbyterian church*, ed. Jean Agnew (Belfast, 1995), p. 46.

37 Recited lease, Wm Robert Adair to Francis Joy, 31 Mar. 1750, in case of Adair v. W. Courtney (PRONI, Adair papers, D/929/HA12/F4/3/1). Lease, Registry of Deeds, vol 166, p. 335, no. 111770.

38 Lease, Sir Robert Adair to William Pettycrew, 1 Nov. 1741 (PRONI, Adair papers, D/929/F2/3/37).

39 Lease, Francis Joy to John Saull, 15 Apr. 1752, Registry of Deeds, vol 387, p.132, no.259445.

40 Lease, Francis Joy to Henry Scott, 9 Mar.1750 (PRONI, Adair papers, D/929/HA12/F4/3/1).

41 W.A. McCutcheon, *The industrial archaeology of Northern Ireland* (Belfast, 1980), p. 253.

42 Indenture, 5 Feb.1740, Registry of Deeds, vol 111, p. 57, no. 75607.

43 *Ordnance Survey Memoirs of Ireland, parishes of Co. Antrim VI,* eds. Angelique Day & Patrick McWilliams (Belfast, 1993), vol 19, p. 53.

44 Mary McNeill, *The life and times of Mary Ann McCracken* (Blackstaff Press edition, Belfast, 1988), pp. 14-15. R.R. Madden, *The United Irishmen and their lives and times* (2nd series, 2 vols, London, 1843) ii, 'Memoir of Henry Joy McCracken': for which Francis Joy's granddaughter Mary Ann McCracken was given as the source of information on the Joy family.

45 Henry Joy, jun., 'Extracts from curious manuscripts' and family notes (LHL, Joy MSS, 6, pp. 366,368); notes on Norton and Ellis families (Joy MSS, 10).
46 *Belfast News Letter,* 4 Mar. 1739/40.
47 Indenture, 19 Jan. 1741, Registry of Deeds, vol 107, p. 32, no. 73078.
48 Robert Munter, *Dictionary of the print trade in Ireland 1550–1775* (New York, 1988), p. 178.
49 Lease, William Robert Adair to Francis Joy, 31 Mar.1750, Registry of Deeds, vol 166, p.335, no.111770.
50 *Belfast News Letter,* 10 May 1757.
51 Lease, Francis Joy to William Courtney, 9&10 Jan. 1760, Registry of Deeds, vol 207, p. 25, no. 135061.
52 Indenture, 10 Jan.1741, Registry of Deeds, vol 107, p. 32, no. 73078.
53 Deed of mortgage, Francis Joy to Archibald McNeill, 29 Apr.1742, Registry of Deeds, vol 119, p. 82, no. 81669.
54 Isaac Ward ('Belfastiensis'), 'The old Irish paper mills', *Belfast Evening Telegraph*, 13 Nov. 1906, p. 6.
55 *J.H.C.I.*, iv, p. 526–7.
56 *Belfast News Letter,* 18 July 1746.
57 *J.H.C.I.*, v, p. 17.
58 *Belfast News Letter,* 1 Jan. 1754.
59 Ibid., 26 Mar. 1765.
60 Ibid., 28 Apr. 1769.
61 Francis Joy to son-in-law John McCracken, 26 May 1760 (inserted in R. M. Young's own extra-illustrated copy of *The town book of Belfast*, Ulster Museum, 440–1931); paper is water-marked 'F JOY'.
62 Isaac Ward ('Belfastiensis'), 'The Joy family and the first Belfast newspaper' in *Belfast Evening Telegraph*, 26 Nov. 1898, p. 6.
63 *Belfast News Letter,* 28 Apr. 1769.
64 Lease, Francis Joy to Henry Ellis, 15&16 May 1780, Registry of Deeds, vol 332, p. 148, no. 223771.
65 *Belfast News Letter,* 22 June 1764, 16 Oct. 1764, 11 Dec. 1764.
66 Ibid., 2 Nov 1750, 8 Nov. 1771, 8 Jan 1773.
67 Deed poll of articles of agreement, Francis Joy to Hugh Carmichael, 19 Nov. 1759; affidavit of Thomas Wallace, 15 Jan. 1768, Registry of Deeds, vol 254, p. 483, no. 169162.
68 Lease, Charles O'Neill to Francis Joy, 11&12 June 1758, Registry of Deeds, vol 222, p. 166, no.147512.
69 *Belfast News Letter,* 24 May 1757.
70 Lease, Charles O'Neill to Francis Joy, 11&12 June 1758, Registry of Deeds, vol 222, p. 166, no.147512. The names of the two former occupiers are illegible.
71 *Belfast News Letter,* 25–29 Mar. 1774.
72 Ibid., 24-27 Feb. 1778, 6–9 Apr. 1779.
73 Ibid., 8-12 Oct. 1790.

74 Ibid., 25–28 July 1794.
75 Ibid., 17 Feb. 1815.
76 Munter, *Dictionary of the print trade in Ireland,* p. 30.
77 George Benn, *History of Belfast* (Belfast, 1877), p. 431–2.
78 Lantern slide photograph, *c.* 1894 of *Belfast Courant*, 22 Apr. 1746 (Ulster Museum, History Department photographic collection, Y14137).
79 *Belfast News Letter,* 7–10 Oct. 1777, 20-24 June 1783.
80 Lease, Donegall to Daniel Blow, 1 June 1754, Registry of Deeds, vol 165, p. 563, no. 113352. Lease, Donegall to Daniel Blow, 21 Sept. 1784, Registry of Deeds, vol 384, p. 421, no. 255773.
81 Lease, Daniel Blow to Nathaniel Wilson, 5 Jan. 1787, Registry of Deeds, vol 384, p. 420, no. 255772. *Belfast News Letter,* 6–9 Oct. 1789.
82 Munter, *Dictionary of the print trade in Ireland,* p. 29.
83 Assignment, John Moore and Martha Moore to Daniel Blow, 10 Mar. 1747/8, transcription from Registry of Deeds, vol 130, p. 130, no. 88254 (PRONI: T/808, p. 885). Lease, Donegall to Daniel Blow, 2 May 1747, Registry of Deeds, vol 128, p. 346, no. 87130.
84 Dubourdieu, *Statistical survey of Co. Antrim*, ii, pp. 413–4.
85 Phillips, *Printing and bookselling in Dublin*, p. 165.
86 *Belfast News Letter,* 23 Mar. 1810.
87 Earl of Harrington to Duke of Bedford transmitting petition from linen drapers of Belfast, 15 Mar. 1747/8 (PRONI: transcription of SPI , T/1060/2 p. 95).
88 *Belfast News Letter,* 7 July 1758.
89 Lease, Donegall to Daniel Blow, 1 June 1754, Registry of Deeds, vol 165, p. 563, no. 113352.
90 *Letter book of Greg & Cunningham 1756–1757, Merchants of New York and Belfast,* ed. Thomas M Truxes (Oxford, 2001), pp. 112, 117n, 148, 203.
91 *Belfast News Letter*, 12 Feb. 1760.
92 Munter, *Dictionary of the print trade in Ireland,* p. 29.
93 J.H.R. Greeves, 'Two Irish Printing Families' in *Belfast Natural History & Philosophical Society*, 2nd series, iv (1955), pp. 38–44.
94 *Belfast News Letter*, 4–7 Jan.1780, 25–28 Apr. 1780, 17–20 Oct. 1780.
95 Bills, 1793 (National Archives Dublin, Rebellion papers, 620/15/8/15/13: microfilm).
96 J.H.R. Greeves, 'Two Irish Printing Families', p. 40.
97 A.P. Woolrich, 'The travel diaries of Joshua Gilpin, some paper mills in Ireland, 1796' in *The Quarterly*, Journal of the British Association of Paper Historians, no. 22 (Apr. 1977), p. 12.
98 PRONI: transcript, T/1009/114.
99 'An account of paper manufacturers who were charged only £16 13 4 per engine instead of £20 16 8 since 25 March 1800 to 25 October following' in Excise Statistics, Ireland, 1746–1822 (3 vols bound in 1 vol, National Archives London, CUST 112/11, i, p. 52).

100 *Belfast News Letter,* 1 June 1802.
101 Ibid., 4 Dec. 1750, 13 Mar. 1753.
102 PRONI, Shaftesbury Estate papers: D/652/26; Donegall Estate papers: D/509/256.
103 PRONI, Donegall Estate papers: D/509/255,257,258.
104 Lease, 29 Aug. 1767 (PRONI, transcription: T/811/vol 2, p. 198).
105 Map, 'A Plan of the River Lagon, and the intended navigable canal from Belfast to Loughneagh. Surveyed by Order of the Rt. Hon. and Hon. the Navigation Board of Ireland in 1768 by Robt. Whitworth, Enginr.' (Ulster Museum, History Department collections, P.19–1981).
106 *Belfast News Letter,* 28 Apr. 1769.
107 Ibid., 20 June 1769.
108 Ibid., 18 Aug. 1769.
109 Ibid., 13 Oct. 1769.
110 Ibid., 19–23 Jan. 1795.
111 PRONI, D/971/M1/14B.
112 *Belfast News Letter,* 28 May–1 June 1779.
113 PRONI, Donegall Estate papers: D/509/607.
114 PRONI, Donegall Estate papers: D/509/603,673,705.
115 Belfast Charitable Society Committee Books: no.4, 1775–1776; no.5, 1776–1779; no.6, 1779–1783 (Belfast, Linen Hall Library): text blocks watermarked: 'HR'[dipthong] 'JOY / BELFAST' with Hibernia in Circle.
116 R.W.M. Strain, *Belfast and its Charitable Society* (Oxford, 1961), *passim.*
117 Michael Bruce to Henry Joy, Dublin, 3 Dec. 1778 (LHL, Joy MSS, 13).
118 Michael Bruce to Henry Joy, Dublin, 11 Sep. 1778 (LHL, Joy MSS, 13).
119 'Commonplace book of Henry Joy of Belfast, tours made by him' (LHL, Joy MSS, 8, pp. 30–31).
120 'Belfastiensis', 'The Joy family and the first Belfast newspaper'.
121 John Gray, 'A tale of two newspapers: the contest between the Belfast News Letter and the Northern Star in the 1790s' in (eds) John Gray & Wesley McCann, *An uncommon bookman, essays in memory of J.R.R. Adams* (Belfast, 1996), pp. 175–180.
122 Notes of Prerogative will of Henry Joy, dated 8 April 1788 (PRONI, transcripts, T/732/43). Notes of Prerogative will of Robert Joy, dated 18 Mar 1785 (PRONI, transcripts, T/732/41).
123 *The Drennan-McTier Letters 1776-1793*, ed. Jean Agnew (3 vols, Dublin 1998), i, p. 453.
124 *Northern Star*, 17–20 Nov. 1794.
125 Assignment, 25th April 1795 (PRONI, transcription: T/811/vol 2, p.203).
126 *Belfast News Letter*, 4–11, 8–11 May 1795.
127 Woolrich, 'The travel diaries of Joshua Gilpin', p. 12.
128 *Belfast News Letter*, 8 Dec. 1797.

129 'An account of the produce of the paper duty in the Excise Distr. in the year ending 25th March 1806' in Excise Statistics, Ireland, 1746–1822 (N.A.L., CUST 112/11, i, p. 105).
130 Assignment of lease, 14 July 1810 (PRONI, D/491/190 & 232).
131 *Belfast News Letter*, 28 Dec. 1792–1 Jan. 1793.
132 Ibid., 11–14 Mar. 1788.
133 Notes of Prerogative will of Henry Joy, dated 8 Apr. 1788 (PRONI, transcripts, T/732/43).
134 *Belfast News Letter*, 1–5 May 1789, 22–25 May 1789, 16–19 Feb. 1790.
135 Ibid., 4–8 Feb. 1791.
136 Citation in re-lease, 25 Mar.1798, Registry of Deeds, vol 514 , p. 199, no. 336024.
137 *Northern Star* minutes 1791–1793 notebook (N.A.D., Rebellion papers, 620/15/8/1, p. 8).
138 *Belfast News Letter*, 28 Dec. 1792–1 Jan. 1793.
139 The Ulster Museum has unbound copies of the *Northern Star* in which the whole watermarks across the centrefolds can be seen, and thus recognised in the bound sets held at the Linen Hall Library, Belfast and Belfast Central Newspaper Library.
140 Mary Pollard, *A dictionary of members of the Dublin book trade 1550–1800* (London, 2000), p. 381.
141 Accounts from Darby McDonnell to *Northern Star*, 5 Mar. 1793 (N.A.D., Rebellion papers, 620/15/8/15/21).
142 Letter and accounts from William Gilbert to John Rabb, May, June & July 1793 (N.A.D., Rebellion papers, 620/15/8/15/17).
143 Pollard, *A dictionary of members of the Dublin book trade*, p. 238.
144 *Northern Star*, 28 Nov.–2 Dec. 1793.
145 Affidavit of Joseph Wall, Nov.[?] 1793 (N.A.D., Rebellion papers, 620/15/8/152).
146 Samuel Neilson to Henry Joy, 16 Apr. 1794 (N.A.D., Rebellion papers, 620/15/8/16/7).
147 *Northern Star*, 10 Nov. 1794.
148 Promissory notes, 1795 (N.A.D., Rebellion papers, 620/15/8/17/21, 22, 28, 33, 36, 39, 40, 47, 48).
149 Promissory notes, 1795 (N.A.D., Rebellion papers, 620/15/8/17/37, 41).
150 *Northern Star* Office, *Bolg an tSolair:* or, *Gaelic Magazine* (Belfast, 1795), (Ulster Museum, History Department, 1974–52).
151 Release, 25 Mar. 1798, Registry of Deeds, vol 514 , p. 199, no. 336024.
152 *Belfast News Letter*, 16 Mar. 1798.
153 'An account of paper manufacturers who were charged only £16 13 4 per engine instead of £20 16 8 since 25 March 1800 to 25 October following' in Excise Statistics, Ireland, 1746–1822 (N.A.L., CUST 112/11, i, p. 52).
154 *Belfast News Letter* 3 Jan. 1806, 11 Apr. 1806, 15 Apr.1806, *Belfast Commercial Chronicle*, 22 Nov. 1806.

155 *Belfast News Letter*, 17 Feb. 1809.
156 Ibid., 2 Dec. 1806.
157 Ibid., 13 Oct. 1815.
158 A Atkinson, *Ireland exhibited to England* (2 vols, London, 1823), ii, p. 145.
159 John J. Marshall, 'Notes on old Belfast printers' in *Quarterly Notes*, Belfast Municipal Museum & Art Gallery publication 107, no. 52 (June 1934), p. 17.
160 Henry Joy jun., notes and letters (LHL, Joy MSS, 10).
161 *Belfast News Letter*, 6 Oct. 1767.
162 Henry Joy jun., note on the geneology of the Raineys, Nov. 1814 (LHL, Joy MSS,10). *Belfast News Letter*, 29 Oct. 1754.
163 Pollard, *Dictionary of Members of the Dublin Book Trade*, p. 143.
164 *Belfast News Letter*, 5 May 1765.
165 *Ibid.*, 23 Dec. 1768.
166 Lease, George Carson to Henry Thetford, 2 July 1784, Registry of Deeds, vol 364 , p. 123, no. 243415.
167 *Belfast News Letter*, 4–8 July 1791.
168 Extract from *Londonderry Journal*, 14 Feb. 1773, reproduced in *Derry Journal* 200th Anniversary issue, Feb. 1972.
169 *Belfast News Letter*, 19-22 Jan. 1779.
170 Title deeds to a papermill and farm in Lettermuck, 1831 (PRONI, D/2446/1).
171 Samuel Lewis, *A topographical dictionary of Ireland* (2nd edit., London, 1847), p. 36.
172 *Ordnance Survey Memoirs of Ireland, parishes of Co. Antrim XI,* (eds) Angelique Day & Patrick McWilliams (Belfast, 1995), vol 29, pp. 15–16.
173 Indenture, 19 Jan. 1741, Registry of Deeds, vol 107, p. 32, no. 73078.
174 *Belfast News Letter*, 10–14 Sep. 1790.
175 *Northern Star* 15–18 Feb. 1792.
176 'An account of paper manufacturers who were charged only £16 13 4 per engine instead of £20 16 8 since 25 March 1800 to 25 October following' in Excise Statistics, Ireland, 1746–1822 (N.A.L., CUST 112/11, i, p. 52).
177 *Belfast News Letter*, 30 Jan. 1797.
178 *Ibid.*, 27–30 Sept. 1785, 5 Aug. 1791, 17 Nov. 1797, 12 Jan. 1802, 27 May 1806, *Northern Star* 10 Nov. 1794.
179 *Ordnance Survey Memoirs of Ireland, parishes of Co. Londonderry XII,* (eds) Angelique Day, Patrick McWilliams & Lisa English (Belfast, 1995), vol 33, p. 130.
180 T.H. Mullin, *Families of Ballyrashane* (Belfast, 1969), p. 180.
181 *Belfast News Letter*, 4 Jan. 1757, 28 Oct. 1777, 11 Aug. 1794.
182 Rent account book, Abercorn estate records, Manor of Cloghogle 1794-1809 (PRONI, D/623/C/4/5, p. 264).

183 Table: 'A view of the Paper Duties in Ireland in the year ending 25 December 1799 and year to 25 March 1803' in Excise Statistics, Ireland, 1746–1822 (N.A.L., CUST 112/11, i, p. 64). The table is clearly inscribed '1791', but as paper duties did not begin until 1798, this is presumed to be a clerical error for '1799'.

184 Ibid.

185 'An account of the produce of the paper duty in the Excise Distr. in the year ending 25th March 1806' in Excise Statistics, Ireland, 1746–1822 (Nat. Arch., London, CUST 112/11, i, p. 105).

186 'An account of the existing rate of duty … on the several articles … chargeable with a duty of excise …' in Excise Statistics, Ireland, 1746–1822 (N.A.L., CUST 112/11, i, p. 73). 'An account of the several additional duties of Excise charged in Ireland by any Act or Acts of Parliament of the UK since the 1st January 1801 … to the 5th January 1813' in Excise Statistics, Ireland, 1746–1822 (N.A.L., CUST 112/11, ii, p. 49). Alterations to paper excise class definitions and rates in Ireland occurred with confusing frequency during the first decade after their introduction.

187 *A map of the cross and bye branching mail coach post roads of Ireland …*, William Larkin, 1806 (Ulster Museum, History Department, postal history collections).

Standing – John Walsh, Dr John Lynch, Patrick Brogan, Norman Johnston, Dr Patrick Fitzgerald, Philip McKelvey, Professor Mary McAleese, Ken Williams, Eric Montgomery O.B.E.
Sitting – Brian O'Hanlon, Gillian Mayes, Deirdre Gillespie.

Reflections on teaching Irish Migration Studies

PATRICK FITZGERALD

THE ABOVE PHOTOGRAPH was taken on the evening of Monday 11 November 1996. Pictured are the eight students who had just embarked upon their first year of study of an MSSc. in Irish Migration Studies. Also pictured are the lecturers charged with delivering the course, Dr John Lynch then of the Department of Economic and Social History, Queen's University Belfast and Dr Patrick Fitzgerald, of the Ulster-American Folk Park. Officially launching the new course on behalf of the university was Professor Mary McAleese, then Pro-Vice Chancellor responsible for outreach. Finally, on the extreme right was Mr Eric Montgomery, former Chief Executive of the Ulster-American Folk Park who had always harboured an aspiration that the Folk Park site should become a centre for scholarship and learning about emigration as well as a popular visitor attraction. On reflection, being in a position to offer a two year part-time postgraduate course in the early autumn of 1996 was remarkable, given that the project had only really been hatched during the previous spring. Discussions between the Ulster-American Folk Park and Queen's University, and particularly between John Gilmour, Folk Park Director and Gary Sloan, who oversaw the university's developing outreach initiative, led to a commitment from both parties to work in partnership towards the establishment of a taught course dealing with emigration.

John Lynch and I were thereafter left to shape the programme and deliver it. My research interest in migration stemmed back to my doctorate which had been concerned in part with Irish vagrancy, subsistence migration and transportation in the early modern period. John had come to migration studies through his own doctoral dissertation, a comparative study of working class life in Belfast, Dublin and Bristol between 1880 and 1925. Whilst it has fallen to me to write this article the whole project has been based on a partnership and none of what I am describing would have been in existence without John's contribution. In setting up the course we should also acknowledge the support of the late David Johnson and Liam Kennedy from the Department of Economic and Social History. Thus in September 1996, with our eight intrepid pioneers aboard, we set out on a journey and now eight years later the editor of *Familia* has asked me to reflect upon this experience.

It probably makes sense to set out the basic shape of the course and try to identify those features which we believe have been central to its success. At the very outset, knowing that we would be delivering a two year part-time Masters, we had to define what precisely we would be studying. In 1995 the key resources of a specialist library collection and a computer database or virtual archive known as the Irish Emigration Database, housed in a splendid new building opened in 1993, were designated as a Centre for Emigration Studies. It might have seemed obvious that we should offer a Masters degree in Irish *Emigration* Studies, but a relatively brief discussion soon drew us towards a somewhat different and broader path. Rather than focussing exclusively upon the single dimension of outward migration it seemed more sensible to deal with the entire phenomenon of human migration in relation to the island of Ireland. Studying in a holistic way movement into, within and out of Ireland offered us, we felt, a more interesting and intellectually satisfying approach. Like many ideas this one became more compelling with time and I will discuss some of the particular merits of this approach presently. The next obvious question to address was whether we should deal with migration in a chronological or thematic way, or indeed, through a combination of the two. This decision took a little longer to reach. Both John and I could see the strengths and weaknesses of all three options but decided in the end to shape the course around an evolving chronology. Having made that decision we obviously needed to define the limits of our chronology. This, oddly for two historians, emerged rapidly. Knowing that we would be delivering four separate modules over two years, the symmetry of four centuries (1600–2000) in four modules appealingly suggested itself. Having committed ourselves to the study of immigration as well as emigration the notion of starting with the seventeenth century, crudely 'the century of immigration', added weight to the proposition. We would begin in 1600 and with the millennium looming there seemed no good reason to truncate our study at any point before the present. Thus we decided from the outset that we should address contemporary migration issues. Undoubtedly this was an emerging strength, as the island, north and south, sought increasingly to come to grips with the issue of immigration from the mid-1990s on. Thus we had four, twelve session modules, dealing in turn with migration into, within and from the island of Ireland during the periods 1600–1700, 1700–1815, 1815–1870 and 1870-present. In 2001 we revised the structure by extending the third module to 1920 and the fourth module accordingly to increase our scope for consideration of contemporary migration issues. (Fuller detail of the lecture schedule can be obtained from the CMS website, www.qub.ac.uk/cms/). This move also was a response to feedback from our students who had expressed a particular interest in issues of contemporary immigration.

This then was the basic structure of the course. What, having delivered it over the course of the last eight years, would I say its particular merits were? Firstly, I would suggest that the idea of dealing holistically with all of the dimensions of migration was a profound advantage. Studying the early eighteenth century emigration of those who were disproportionately Ulster Presbyterians, made greater sense when students had a survey of British immigration to Ireland in the seventeenth century already 'under their belts'. More topically one might highlight the potential insights drawn from parallel consideration of those who left the Republic of Ireland in the depressed 1980s and lived and worked illegally in the United States, alongside immigrants of various types and backgrounds who came to the Ireland of the 'Celtic Tiger' economy. Consideration too of the relationship between internal migration and emigration is enlightening at a number of levels. This point perhaps becomes clearer when one focuses upon the individual migrant. Where the historical record permits us to reconstruct the complete migration profile of any individual, we can often discern the connections between migration within Ireland and subsequent emigration where that occurred. David Fitzpatrick's work on Irish-Australian correspondence has demonstrated how a detailed and nuanced understanding of the Irish local context from which emigrants were drawn adds greatly to the depth of our understanding about their subsequent migration experience and behaviour [D. Fitzpatrick, *Oceans of Consolation: Personal Accounts of Irish Migration to Australia* (Cork, 1995)].

Secondly, the fact that we were taking a relatively 'long view' of Irish migration history had distinct merits. I say 'relatively' because I know that to the historians of early Ireland, not to mention those studying the prehistoric and early historic periods, our long view might be considered a mere snapshot. Nonetheless, today historical research and writing often tend to be quite narrowly 'period specific', and bridging the early modern, modern, contemporary history divides can provide an illuminating perspective, allowing students to make connections and comparisons in a temporal as well as a spatial dimension. We don't, for example, often set into a comparative frame or establish any connection between Scottish migrants to Ireland in the seventeenth century and Irish migrants to Scotland in the nineteenth century. Yet, in fact, the peaks in the volume of both movements coincided with devastating famine. Equally we might not automatically think of the parallels between those filing applications for asylum in Ireland today with groups like the Huguenots and Palatinates who, as continental European Protestant refugees, were given asylum from religious persecution in later seventeenth and early eighteenth century Ireland. This latter association, indeed, was one fruitfully explored in a dissertation by one of our students.

A third feature of the course which has evolved since 1996 and which I think enhances what individual students gain from migration studies, is a focus on their own lives and the exploration of their own 'migration profiles'. At the outset of the course we introduce the idea that we all have a migration profile or migration story and in one particular tutorial exercise we focus specifically on the lived experiences of our students as migrants, in order to try to better understand the essential, universal components of being a migrant. Understanding and reflecting upon one's own experience can sharpen the appreciation of the complexity of making decisions about moving or staying, about the problems and challenges of leaving and arriving, about settling in to a new place and constructing an ongoing relationship with home. Some of the students draw upon their own experiences and life skills in deciding the subject of their own research dissertations and the fact that migration studies embraces many disciplines itself can permit students to consider a variety of approaches. Although less explicitly an objective of the course, we nonetheless regard it as a positive outcome when students tell us that their study has connected with them at a personal level and given them a fresh perspective on their own past and present.

Inevitably given the predominance of emigration in Irish history much of the course is concerned with migration out of Ireland and what used to be described as the Irish abroad or the Irish overseas. I say 'used to' because during the period that the course has been running there has been a very significant development in the way we think about the outcome of Irish emigration globally. Since the early 1990s the concept of an Irish Diaspora has become increasingly influential. The use of the term by Mary Robinson as Irish President, has done much to increase popular resonance with the term both at home and abroad. To a greater extent than was the case in 1996 we encourage analysis of an interconnected entity across the centuries and across the planet. Each individual migrant, of whom there were some 10 million in total between 1600 and 2004, has become a part of the Irish Diaspora which today has in excess of 70 million members. Though we may focus on migrants in a particular destination in a particular period, it is the context and connectivity of the Irish Diaspora which serves to establish a meaningful framework. This dimension of the course and the imperative to set Irish patterns into a wider comparative frame is something one is conscious of expanding within the curriculum in the future.

One further observation I might make relates to the fact that many of the students are mature students returning to formal education after many years. Some have described the course as a chance to reacquaint themselves with Irish history and to view it through a fresh prism – that of migration. Given that each fresh intake of students has drawn from across the community divide, and indeed the border, one might suggest that the course and particularly the forum of tutorial discussion provides a suitable yet comfortable arena to adjust the generalities or popular stereotypes of traditional, dominant Unionist or Nationalist narratives. In addition, I suspect that the exploration of differences on the island of Ireland, off the island of Ireland as it were, eases the pressure of debating differences frankly but tolerantly. One was certainly heartened to note that students who were approached in 2001 for feedback for a Department of Culture, Arts and Leisure evaluation of CMS, considered that the course made an important contribution to a growing appreciation of cultural diversity and served to enhance mutual understanding. Conscious of the risk of beginning to sound like yet another corporate promo I will move on!

Thus far readers may have gained some idea of the outline structure of the course but little appreciation of how this exploration progresses in practice. In order to try to give some indication of how the course 'works' let me say something more about the structure of a typical session and about the components of assessment deployed. Each of the forty-eight taught sessions is delivered in the Centre for Migration Studies at the Ulster-American Folk Park on a Monday evening from late September through to early December and then from late January through to early May. Students generally arrive into the Centre from late afternoon on, doing some private study, conducting business with the Library staff or meeting with John or myself. The session commences officially at 6.30 pm when we split into first and second year groups, with John or myself taking either group. Generally the students are never 'subjected' to more than three consecutive sessions with the same tutor which we consider to be healthy. John and I are sufficiently different in style and in perspective to hopefully offer a stimulating contrast. In short, John would see himself primarily as an economic historian and a modernist whilst I would see myself more as a social historian and an early modernist. Personal inclination and limited time curtailed any effort to 'read off the same hymn sheet'. Where students have confronted either of us with the alternative argument or evidence of the other we take it as a thoroughly healthy sign (a) that they are actually listening to us and (b) that they are conscious of the contested debate that history represents. The tutor then delivers a lecture on the subject matter of the session, lasting around 45-60 minutes and this is followed by questions raised by the lecture.

At around 7.45–8.00 both groups break for ten minutes or so for a cup of tea/coffee and then reconvene for a tutorial session. The tutorial, which generally concludes between 9.00 and 9.30, varies in design. Generally the students are responding to material we have circulated the previous week. I often produce a pack of documents, including maps, images, cartoons etc. and ask one student to be prepared to lead discussion on each particular item of evidence. When dealing with emigration from the eighteenth century on, particularly to North America, the Centre's Irish Emigration Database is a great boon. Containing keyword searchable digitised transcriptions of more than 32,000 relevant archival documents, it is relatively straightforward to bring together documents pertinent to the tutorial subject. On other occasions the tutorial can take a different format. For example, I have mentioned the exercise where we explore our own migration profiles, in addition we use role play scenarios where appropriate. John, for example, tackles the complex decade of the 1640s in this way whilst I have applied this method to twentieth century emigration. At its best this method of learning can be supremely successful. Without picking out names and dates I recall one group in which each student had been presented with an individual migrant scenario and asked to adopt the persona of the migrant and discuss the decisions they had made and their projections for the future. They would then take questions from the group. The quality of all of the contributions was exceptional, the capacity to empathise with the migrants very real but balanced by perceptive analysis of their behaviour and situation. Whilst most of our sessions are held at the Centre for Migration Studies, we occasionally 'migrate' to Omagh Technology Centre, where we are able, with the support of the Western Education and Library Board staff, to engage in video conference exchanges. Being able to import a guest lecture from thousands of miles away and then to get into discussion with those studying migration elsewhere is a great advantage. Over the past number of years we have been involved in conferences with Prof. Bruce Elliott and his students at Carleton University in Canada and Dr Marjory Harper and her students at the University of Aberdeen. Their students hopefully get something from what I present and I know our students gain from what Bruce and Marjory have contributed. This form of teaching is unlikely ever to replace face to face contact, but it is valuable as reasonably affordable added value and good experience for all students and teachers. In the future one can see the potential for this technology to help make Irish Migration Studies a viable distance learning course. I have already had prospective students from Britain, North America, Queensland and Tasmania enquiring about such a possibility.

Readers who might feel tempted by migration studies may want to know a little more about how their performance is measured, the hurdles to be jumped before graduating. At present each of the four modules is assessed on the basis of three components. Half the marks are drawn from coursework, ten per cent on the basis of tutorial contributions as assessed by the tutor and the remaining forty per cent on the basis of a set essay submitted in the penultimate week of the module. The remaining fifty per cent of the module mark derives from a two hour examination held a few weeks after the taught module concludes. The four taught modules account for two thirds of the course assessment with the final third accounted for by a 15–20,000 word dissertation based on the students' research and submitted in the September of the second year.

As I have already indicated migration studies is a broad field and really multidisciplinary and comparative by nature, so students have a fairly wide range of issues, topics and approaches open to them. Obviously it is the task of the tutors as supervisors and ultimately the external examiner to ensure that the study of migration is central to the work. John and I have generally left students to come up with their own proposals rather than direct them to our research agenda. Obviously where a student is struggling to identify an enticing and viable project we will offer advice as to what might constitute a good research project. The advantage of the dissertation subject being generated by the student is that they feel a stronger sense of ownership of the dissertation from the outset. It also enhances the chances of them selecting a subject they are really interested in or feel connected to. Again here the relationship between their own migration and life experience and their research and analysis can be a positive benefit as long, of course, as they maintain sufficient academic distance. Reflecting upon the significant body of work now produced by students and housed in the Centre for Migration Studies library and conscious of all the 'late night oil' burned in producing it and still being burned creating those in production, both myself and John remain profoundly proud of the efforts of all those students.

The final element in the course which I could not fail to mention is the fieldtrip which makes up a fully integrated element of each module. Thus, since 1996, I and/or John have led some 46 fieldtrips to venues as close as the Ulster History Park, between Omagh and Gortin and as distant as Tralee and Cork. As a student myself, I was fortunate enough to have benefited from the initiative of Peter Jupp in the Department of History at Queen's, in obtaining the resources necessary to take students out into the field. I learned from this the advantages of seeing sites and meeting 'locals' in trying to make sense of the past.

Some day it would be great to take a fieldtrip to Montserrat, Newfoundland or Manhattan but exploring migration history in Ireland serves to remind us of the close link between local studies and migration studies. The idea of a townland, parish or county diaspora seems a good deal less incongruous when you are walking through a graveyard, observing the remnants of a clachan in a field, talking to local experts or simply chatting to local people in a pub during the evening. Wherever you travel in Ireland you are soon reminded of the pervasive influence of chain migration. There was little sporadic or random about the developing patterns of emigration from Ireland. The fieldtrips are about study and engagement with migration but they are also fun. Fortunately my word limit precludes me from recounting numerous fieldtrip anecdotes but I hope that all our former students found these excursions a part of lifelong learning in the broadest sense.

The MSSc. students studying in Omagh are, of course, full students of Queen's University and entitled to use all the university's libraries and other facilities. In the Centre for Migration Studies, however, they enjoy the special benefit of a specialist library collection of some 11,000 volumes relating to Irish migration and the use of a virtual archive, the Irish Emigration Database currently containing over 32,000 documents. These facilities are made accessible to students through the Centre's library staff. Chris McIvor, the Librarian, who herself graduated from the course with distinction a few years ago, Christine Johnston, Senior Library Assistant and Joe Mullan, our ICT officer all offer intensive guidance on the Monday evenings and help run the course in innumerable ways. The late John Winters, who was previously our Database Manager, likewise contributed much in his time to the course and particularly some of those early video conference sessions. We should also acknowledge the support of the Scotch-Irish Trust for Ulster. They support the course in a very practical way through a Bursary scheme to which students may apply in case of financial hardship. I should also like to acknowledge the particular role of the CMS Director, Dr. Brian Lambkin who has, since taking up that post in 1998, contributed enormously to the success of the course. Since that date he has challenged me to think both about what I am teaching and how I am teaching and through his own steadfast commitment and integrity made my job a lot fuller but a lot easier.

Overall, the eight years the course has been running have flown by and I reflect upon the rewards of attracting very committed students. That they have been prepared to travel to Omagh on 48 Monday nights over two years from places as distant and diverse as Sligo, Cavan, Dundalk, Newtownards, Glengormley, Ballymena, Castlenock or Ramelton, demonstrates this alone. It is a real pleasure to see many of our former students return to CMS every February for our reunion lecture and keep in touch with developments in the field and meet up with old friends. I can honestly say that I have enjoyed being involved with all the students who have joined the course and gained a tremendous amount personally from our collective exploration of four centuries of Irish migration history. Back in 1996 we had no real means of knowing who we would attract and how long we could sustain the course. To have had more than seventy students who have produced some really top quality work is very pleasing. In September 2004, a further intake of eleven students was installed and we very much hope that we continue to recruit well in the years ahead. Perhaps, looking further into the future we can look forward to a time where the new technology may be utilised more fully to make the course available to those in the global Irish Diaspora and to allow us greater scope for mutual enrichment through engagement with scholars and students exploring the history of human migration in its entirety.

Reconstructing an eighteenth-century Ulster family:

the Reas of Magheraknock and Killeen, County Down

WILLIAM ROULSTON

AS ANYONE KNOWS who has attempted to search for their ancestors, finding out reliable information about them before 1800 is often far from straightforward. The loss of so many records in the destruction of the Public Record Office of Ireland in 1922, coupled with less systematic record-keeping has left a legacy of problems that is not easy to overcome. Nonetheless there is a large body of information out there that can be utilised by historical and genealogical researchers. Some of these sources are well known, such as the flax-growers' list of 1796, and the hearth money rolls of the 1660s but many others are not. In particular there is a mass of information contained within collections of estate papers which has not yet been fully exploited. The obvious difficulty with accessing these sources is the lack of a detailed guide to pre-1800 records. The Ulster Historical Foundation is currently engaged in a project to identify sources from the seventeenth and eighteenth centuries of use to local and family historians. The geographical area covered is the nine-county province of Ulster. Hopefully this guide will be published in book form in the first half of 2005. As an example of what can be recovered about an eighteenth-century Ulster family, in this case a Presbyterian family with roots in Scotland, this essay presents a brief study of the Rea family of Magheraknock and Killeen in County Down.

The Reas were not of the landlord class, nor even minor gentry, yet several members of this family carved out for themselves an important place in the historical record both in Ireland and on the other side of the Atlantic in the American colonies. In his classic study, *Ulster Emigration to Colonial America*, R.J. Dickson devotes a section of one chapter to activities of Matthew Rea, as an emigration agent, many of which were undertaken on behalf of his brother, John, who had emigrated to South Carolina about 1729.[1] About Matthew Rea's background, Dickson was forced to admit that he knew very little. More recently Kerby Miller *et al.* have discussed the role of the Rea brothers in bringing settlers to the American colonies[2] as did Michael Morris[3] so it is not necessary to go over this ground again. This short study is focussed on the family in Ireland and highlights what can be discovered about them using a range of contemporary sources. It builds on research carried out prior to 1980 by Mary Osborne.[4] The father of Matthew and John Rea was David Rea and it is with him that a start can be made.

DAVID REA OF MAGHERAKNOCK

The first point of entry into this family was the identification of an abstract of the will of David Rea of Magheraknock. It is a well known fact that virtually all original wills probated before 1858 – when the state took over responsibility for administering wills from the Church of Ireland – were destroyed in Dublin in 1922. A large number of wills, however, had also been registered in the Registry of Deeds in Dublin. The importance of the Registry of Deeds as an archival institution will be discussed presently. Abstracts of the wills in the Registry of Deeds between 1708 and 1832 were published in three volumes by the Irish Manuscripts Commission.

Volume two contains an abstract of the will of a David Rea of Belycreen or, more correctly, Ballycreen, in the parish of Magheradrool County Down.[5] The will was dated 2 February 1754. The testator appointed two of his sons, Mathew and Hugh, to be his executors. He refers to 'my last wife's children she had to me', named as Debro, James, Jane and Robert. The lands of 'Kelein' belonging to the testator and then being held by John and Robert Granger are mentioned as is the holding in Ballycreen also the mill of Magheraknock, both of which were held from Mr Onsley (Annesley). The will was registered by Debro Armstong, 'otherwise Rea now the wife of John Armstrong of Maghrenock, Co. Down, farmer' who, it is reasonable to assume, was one of the daughters of David Rea. Interestingly, the will was registered on 7 November 1774, over twenty years after it was written. While the abstract was helpful, an examination of the copy of the will was made. This was possible using a microfilm in the Public Record Office of Northern Ireland. Nothing of particular significance was discovered that was not already covered in the abstract, although it was noted that the lands of Kelein were to go to the children of his second wife, while his sons Hugh and Matthew were to receive the farm in Ballycreen and Magherynock mill.[6]

GRAVESTONE INSCRIPTIONS

In his will David Rea requested that he be buried in the churchyard of Saintfield. A search was therefore made to see if a gravestone to this man had survived. The Ulster Historical Foundation has published 21 volumes of gravestone inscriptions for County Down and Saintfield is covered in volume three. The churchyard in question is that surrounding the Church of Ireland church in the town, a burial place used, on account of its seventeenth-century origins, by Presbyterians as well as Anglicans. There was indeed a gravestone to David Rea, a horizontal stone on the ground in a modern railed enclosure, and the inscription on this memorial reads as follows:

> Here lyeth ye body of David Rea of Maharynock Hill, who departed this life ye 16 of March 1754, aged 82 years, and also his son Hugh Rea of said place, who departed this life ye 2 of June 1759, aged 42 years, likewise the body of his son David Rea, who departed this life January 3d 1770, aged 13 years, also ye rimains of Elizabeth Rea otherwise Jackson, wife to ye above Hugh Rea, who died October ye 8th 1779, aged 62 years, here lyeth ye body of Cathrin Rea otherwise Barnett, wife of Matthew Rea, who departed ys life ye 2d of January 1781, aged 68 years.

This gravestone therefore provides information on three generations of the Rea family. David Rea died in 1754 aged 82 meaning that he must have been born in 1672 or thereabouts. He would therefore have lived during the troubled times of 1689–91 when the siege of Derry took place and the battles at the Boyne (1690) and at Aughrim (1691) were fought. The gravestone additionally records the death of Hugh Rea, one of the executors to his father's will, and also Hugh's son David who died in his early teens. Hugh's wife Elizabeth, whose maiden name was Jackson, and the wife of Matthew Rea, Catherine, née Barnett are also commemorated. Matthew Rea is not recorded on the memorial, though he was presumably buried in this churchyard. We have no precise information on when he died, but in the index to wills probated in the diocese of Dromore, the will of a Mathew Rea of Ballycreen was discovered. This will was probated in 1800 and may have been that of the emigration agent. The original will was destroyed in Dublin and no duplicate copy or abstract was found in the Public Record Office of Northern Ireland.

BALLYNAHINCH PRESBYTERIAN CHURCH REGISTERS

Although the *Guide to Church Records* compiled by the Public Record Office of Northern Ireland lists the earliest Presbyterian registers from Ballynahinch as dating from no earlier than 1820, recently some very early registers have come to light, a computerised copy of which was presented to the Ulster Historical Foundation. These relate to what is now 1st Ballynahinch Presbyterian Church and cover the period from 1696 to 1735.[7] We found the baptisms of the following children of David Rea:

John bapt. Thursday 12 July 1705
John bapt. Sunday 16 April 1710
Hugh bapt. 26 June 1715
David bapt. 12 December 1717
David bapt. December 1719
Elizabeth bapt. 23 December 1722
Debora bapt. 4 April 1725
James bapt. 23 March 1729

For whatever reason Matthew was not listed among the children. Clearly two of the children died young, hence the duplication of the names John and David (a practice that can often be a source of confusion for present-day genealogists). We can assume that the second John, baptised in 1710, was the man who emigrated to South Carolina, *c.* 1729. The finding of these early registers is remarkable and highly valuable as far as the Rea family is concerned. Who can tell how many more such items still await discovery? Without doubt this discovery is a useful reminder that new genealogical sources are being found on a regular basis enabling new insights into the families of the past to be gained.

REGISTRY OF DEEDS

In 1708 the Registry of Deeds was established in Dublin as a repository for all kinds of documents – including sales, mortgages, leases, and as has already been shown, wills – relating to the legal transfer of title to land. To begin with the Registry was principally used by middle and upper ranking members of the Church of Ireland, though this does not mean that persons of other denominations and from further down the social scale will find no mention in it. By the beginning of the nineteenth century the Registry was being much more widely used and by 1832 more than 500,000 deeds had been registered there. There are two indexes. The first is an index of the grantors' names, the second a place-name index. The indices and memorials are available on microfilm in the Public Record Office of Northern Ireland.[8] A search through the indices revealed a number of potentially interesting items which were then examined in more detail.

Two mortgages from 1739 and 1742 involving David Rea were discovered. The earlier of the two, dated 29 October 1739, was a mortgage of the Quarterland of Killeen – the Kelein of David Rea's will – in the parishes of Holywood and Dundonald for £100.[9] From this deed we learned that David Rea's wife was Elizabeth Martin. The second deed, dated 11 September 1742, was also a mortgage of Killeen, this time for £200.[10] Clearly David Rea was in need of some ready cash, though what he was using the money for is not known. It may have been to purchase additional lands or even to have set one of his sons up in business, though this is merely speculation. The latter deed is particularly interesting in that it refers to David Rea's wife as formerly Martin and identifies one of the parties to the mortgage as John Magill of Ballycroon [sic], a linen weaver, who is stated to have been her eldest son by her former marriage. We can take from this that Elizabeth Rea had been previously married to a man by the name of Magill (by whom she had children) and that Martin was her maiden name.[11] Elizabeth Rea was David Rea's second wife. She was identified, but not named in his will, probably because she had predeceased him. The name of his first wife is not known.

Two deeds from the 1770s throw some light on Matthew Rea, the emigration agent. The first, dated 22 December 1774, involved on the one hand Margaret Rea, widow, and David Rea, farmer, both of Killeen, and on the other hand Mathew Ryan [sic] of Drumbo, gent.[12] The deed was an assignment of a rent charge of £20 *per annum* arising out of the lands of Killeen in the possession of Margaret and David Rea and their under-tenants, John Murray and Thomas Mayne. The deed stated that Margaret was the widow and David the eldest son and heir of the late James Rea of Killeen. This James Rea was the son of David Rea of Magheraknock; his father's will had named him as one of the heirs of the lands of 'Kelein'. Mathew Ryan was obviously Mathew Rea, son of David Rea of Magheraknock, and half-brother of James Rea. His address was given as Drumbo and he was styled 'gent.', implying that he had some social standing. The second deed, dated 9 November 1776, was a transfer of the rent charge from Matthew Rea to Robert Stevenson of Belfast, surgeon and apothecary, and it recited much of the information in the first deed.[13]

By this time, therefore, there were two branches of the Rea family, one living at Magheraknock and the other at Killeen. James Rea was married to Margaret, but we do not know her maiden name. From the Ballynahinch registers we know that James Rea was born in 1729. We have no record of when he died, but clearly it was before December 1774. At this stage David Rea of Killeen would have been a fairly young man – he may not even have reached majority (i.e. over 21). This would explain why his mother was also party to the deed with his uncle Matthew.

The discovery of a deed from the early nineteenth century relating to the Rea family of Killeen throws light on how the family came to be in possession of the townland in the first place. This was a conveyance of 5 July 1810 between David Rea of Killeen, farmer, and Hugh Rea of Killeen, his son, of part of Killeen.[14] The deed refers to a lease of 2 July 1694 by which James Ross of Portavoe, County Down, leased to David Martin of Killeen the Quarterland of Killeen in as ample a manner as Ross had held it from the Earl of Clanbrassil. The rent in 1694 was to be £10 12s. per annum. On the basis of this deed it may be assumed that David Rea held Killeen through his wife Elizabeth Martin given that in 1694 a David Martin was granted Killeen by James Ross. According to Mary Osborne, Elizabeth Rea was the daughter of David Martin.[15] The fact that a deed of 1810 should refer back to a lease of 1694 should not be passed over without some comment. It highlights the value of checking nineteenth-century deeds in the Registry of Deeds for information on seventeenth- and eighteenth-century families.

It is also worth noting that, in the course of researching the Reas in the eighteenth century, an extremely interesting early nineteenth-century deed dated 29 July 1811 between Martin Rea of Killeen, farmer, and Arthur Calley, also a Killeen farmer, was found. It provides, among much else, useful information on the material possessions and culture of a farmer of Rea's status.[16] This deed refers to an earlier lease made on 13 December 1809 between David Rea of Killeen and Martin Rea of a parcel of ground in Killeen. The duration of this lease was 31 years or the lives of Martin Rea and his 14 year old son 'Js' (possibly James). As he was on the point of emigrating to America he wanted to dispose of his possessions and property to Arthur Calley. Accordingly, the deed goes on to recite that Martin Rea had in his possession a horse, cow, pig, cart, farm utensils, three beds and other household furniture in Killeen. The deed also mentions Martin Rea's wife and seven children: Js, Elizabeth, Nancy, Martin, Robert, Sally and John. The witnesses to the deed included David Rea of Belfast. One wonders what happened to Martin Rea when he arrived in America with his large family. Given the age of Martin Rea's son, it is probable that Martin was a brother of David Rea of Killeen rather than a son.

Research in the Registry of Deeds has uncovered an astonishing amount of information about this family and has allowed us to build up a picture of this family over several generations. It has not provided us with all the answers we needed, but it has helped to fill in many of the gaps created by the absence of other sources. It is also worth making the point that the Reas were Presbyterians and, in the main, tenant farmers, and yet such rich material has been unearthed about them in the Registry of Deeds, an archive that continues to be presented as one offering little hope to those searching such families in eighteenth-century Ulster.

ESTATE PAPERS

Estate papers form a vast and vital source of genealogical information, particularly for the eighteenth century when other sources may not be available. David Rea's will of 1754 indicated that he was a tenant on the Annesley estate. There is a large collection of material relating to this estate in the Public Record Office of Northern Ireland. One item in particular was especially revealing about the Rea family. This was a letter-book kept by Edward Moore who was the agent on the Annesley estate in a latter part of the eighteenth century. In this letter-book a letter written by Edward Moore to Arthur Annesley Esq. on 10 July 1776 referred to Matthew Rea. It is included here in full:

> There is one particular farm you will see in [the] Rent Roll under the title of Widow of Hugh Rea, to which two-thirds of Magheranock Mill are added, which I would wish in particular to have surveyed. It is now held by one Matt[he]w Rea, a brother to the above widow's husband, who got into it and holds it not very fairly, as I am informed. As to the payment of his rent, he is punctual, and has made money in exporting our Protestants to America to people the lands of a brother of his and others who went there some time ago, and for whom he was a sort of slave factor [the word 'agent' has here been crossed out]. This man does not live on the lands he holds, but set them to a number of poor people at double rent, as I have reason to believe; and what provoked me most of all was that he to prevent their coming in to bid for the lands, when I called in the proposals sent over last spring, took bonds from them, all with a penalty annexed, in case they bid for their

> lands – this I heard from a neighbouring tenant, and the example appeared to me so black and villainous, that I not only charged him with it, but told him I would represent it. This he answered by threats, that he knew when to apply as well as I did, and would be [-?] with me. I shall leave the rest to your better judgement, Sir, and follow your instructions.[17]

To uncover something like this about a particular individual is a real gem as it brings to life, as it were, the person concerned. In some ways it really does not matter that Matthew Rea turns out not have been the most scrupulous of people – what is important is that we have a fresh perspective on this eighteenth-century Ulsterman and his relationships with some of those around him.

CONCLUSION

This has only been a brief sortie into the world of one Ulster Presbyterian family in the eighteenth century and is certainly not intended as the final word on the Reas of Magheraknock and Killeen. Nor is it intended to make researchers think that the same sort of material can be recovered about every family of similar background and status in the province. The Reas were clearly fairly exceptional. However, what I have hopefully been able to do is demonstrate the worth of carrying out research prior to 1800 and what may be found. By piecing together fragments of evidence it is possible to reconstruct families from the seventeenth and eighteenth centuries and in doing so build up a picture of the social world in which they lived. In this way genealogy has much to offer the social and economic, never mind the local, historian.

NOTES

1 R.J. Dickson, *Ulster Emigration to Colonial America* (Belfast, 1966), pp. 164–73.
2 Kerby A. Miller, Arnold Schrier, Bruce D. Boling, David N. Doyle, *Irish Immigrants in the Land of Canaan: Letters and Memoirs from Colonial and Revolutionary America, 1675–1815* (Oxford University Press, New York, 2003), pp. 82–5.
3 Michael P. Morris, 'Profits and Philanthropy: The Ulster Immigration Schemes of George Galphin and John Rea' in *Journal of Scotch-Irish Studies* (Winter, 2002), pp. 1–11.
4 Mary Jane McMahon Osborne, *Rea, Rae, of Ballynahinch, Holywood, and allied families, County Down, Ulster, Northern Ireland* (1980), copy in PRONI under D/3000/149. The initial research on this family was carried out without prior knowledge of Ms Osborne's work and several of the findings are duplicated. However, on a number of points my discoveries contradict Ms Osborne's interpretation of the family's history. In particular the evidence I have uncovered suggests that David Rea was only married twice, not three times, which has implications for our understanding of the Reas in the latter part of the eighteenth century.
5 P. Beryl Eustace, *Registry of Deeds, Dublin. Abstracts of Wills*, ii (Dublin, 1954), pp. 256–7.
6 The Registry of Deeds reference to the will is 302.571.202079.
7 The registers and other items of interest can be accessed on the internet at http://freepages.genealogy.rootsweb.com/~rosdavies/WORDS/Ballynahinch PresbyterianIndex.htm.
8 MIC/7 for the indexes and MIC/311 for the memorials.
9 Registry of Deeds, 99.17.67715.
10 Registry of Deeds, 109.88.75088.
11 According to Mary Osborne (*op. cit.*, p. 32), Elizabeth Rea married Thomas Magill in 1714 and had three sons by him, David, John and Robert.
12 Registry of Deeds, 305.477.203064.
13 Registry of Deeds, 314.77.210257.
14 Registry of Deeds, 629.89.429764.
15 Osborne, *op. cit.*, p. 32.
16 Registry of Deeds, 637.308.43811.
17 PRONI D/2309/4/3, letter-book, Annesley estate. Several other letters in this document also refer to Matthew Rea.

REVIEWS

PATRICK DUFFY (ED.)

To and from Ireland: Planned Migration Schemes c. 1600–2000

Geography Publications, Dublin, 2004
ISBN 0 906602 378 pp. 209 €20

In recent years the patterns, networks, and processes of Irish migration, emphasising the similarities between Irish migration patterns and those that prevailed more broadly on transatlantic and even global scales, have received more scholarly attention. In *To and from Ireland*, editor Patrick J. Duffy, an historical geographer at NUI-Maynooth, has added to this new literature by bringing together nine essays that focus on planned Irish migrations between the early seventeenth and the mid-twentieth centuries.

The contributors' topics range widely. In the initial chapter after Duffy's introductory essay, Ciaran O'Scea examines the 'overlooked' migration of at least 10,000 Gaelic and Hiberno-Norman Catholic lords and their followers from Munster to Spain in the immediate aftermath of the Nine Years War. Most refugees were impoverished, widowed, or orphaned, and O'Scea's primary emphasis is their cool reception by Spanish officials who – with the honourable exception of the governor of Galicia, where most of the exiles settled – regarded them as a 'useless' burden on the Spanish treasury and tried to repatriate them to Ireland. The next chapter also focuses on the seventeenth century but on the migration to Ireland, especially to the Ulster plantation, of thousands of Protestant Scots and English. According to Raymond Gillespie, the British state created the essential political, legal, social, and religious 'framework to encourage migration,' primarily through its confiscations and redistributions of Irish land. However, the government's efforts to direct or even encourage Protestant migration *per se* were less effective than economic factors and thus serve as 'powerful reminder[s] of the limited capacity of early modern administrators to plan migration.'

As Trevor Parkhill explains in chapter three, by the early 1700s the descendants of earlier Protestant settlers in Ireland were beginning to emigrate to England's North American colonies, after 1776 to the new United States or to what would later be Canada. And in the pre-famine era (1815–1844) roughly one half-million Protestants and an equal (and steadily increasing) number of Catholics left Ireland for North America. During this 'long eighteenth century,' official British opinions of Irish emigration changed radically, from mercantilist opposition to grudging acceptance and even eager encouragement. In the same period, however, élite attitudes toward the state's 'managerial' role changed equally radically, from interventionist to classic liberal doctrines of *laissez faire*. Thus, ironically at the very moment when the British government had acquired both the means and the incentive to relieve Irish poverty (or prevent famine) through tax-supported migration schemes, with one brief exception (in 1821–23) the state abdicated responsibility for assisting emigration to Irish landlords, to colonial governments and land companies, and, primarily, to the private kinship networks of letters and prepaid passages that had become increasingly prevalent after the transatlantic servant trade began to decline in the late 1700s.

As Patrick Duffy contends, by the 1820s–30s the Malthusian notion that 'overpopulation' (especially of Ireland's Catholics) restricted economic, social, and moral 'progress' had become 'fashionable,' and a few Irish landlords had begun to assist tenant migration as part of broader plans to 'modernise' their estates. As Duffy and Thomas Power point out, however, in the fourth and fifth chapters in this collection, it was the combination of the Irish Poor Law (1838) and the Great Famine (1845–52) – the latter by collapsing estate income, the former by imposing high poor rates on the most impoverished estates – that inspired landlords to aid roughly 100,000 people (*c.* 6–8% of all Famine emigrants) to go overseas, principally to British North America. Only a few of Ireland's wealthiest proprietors, especially those with English estates, could afford the costs of assisted mass migration. According to Power, for example, in the first half of 1847 alone Lord

Palmerston spent £5,600 to aid over 1,600 people to leave one of his County Sligo estates. The impact of such schemes in certain localities was enormous: Palmerston sent nearly 4,300 overseas, and his Sligo neighbour, Gore-Booth, shipped another 1,200; likewise, 5,800 people were assisted to emigrate from the Wandesforde estate in north Kilkenny; nearly 6,000 from the Fitzwilliam properties in Wicklow; another 5,000 from the Shirley and Bath estates in Monaghan; some 3,360 out of the Lansdowne estate in Kerry; and so forth. According to Power, most evidence suggests that assisted emigrants were happy to leave, and their remittances enabled roughly double their numbers to depart soon afterward. And, as Power points out, Palmerston could have emulated the majority of his peers and simply evicted his dependents, throwing them out on the road to starve or fend for themselves. Yet Duffy reminds readers also to attend the 'subaltern voices' of the dispossessed, and he cautions that assisted emigration was ultimately an estate-management tool and, for landlords and their agents, the welfare of emigrant tenants (most of whom received only their passage costs and arrived destitute if not disease-ridden) was merely 'a happy coincidence.'

Post-famine assisted emigration is the subject of the sixth essay by Gerard Moran, author of *Sending out Ireland's poor: Assisted emigration to North America in the nineteenth century* (Dublin, 2004). Post-famine schemes, whether officially or privately sponsored, were smaller in scale than those implemented in 1845–52. However, between 1849 and 1906 Irish poor law authorities sent out some 45,000 persons, primarily to Canada; in the early 1860s the Queensland Immigration Society aided over 6,600 to reach Australia; and philanthropist Vere Foster helped thousands of young, single Irishwomen to migrate to North America. The most ambitious post-famine scheme was implemented in the distressed early 1880s, when private charity (spearheaded by Quaker philanthropist James Hack Tuke), Catholic clergymen, the Irish poor law boards, and the British treasury combined to sponsor the migration to North America of some 50,000 people, principally from Galway, Mayo, and other poor western counties. As in 1845–52, generally successful reports were offset by controversies: Irish nationalists denounced what they called the planned 'extermination' of the

'Irish Race' at home; U.S. officials objected to the 'shovelling out' of Irish workhouse inmates onto American shores; and middle-class Irish-Americans were embarrassed by the extreme poverty and 'character' deficiencies allegedly exhibited by many of the 'Connemaras' and other Irish-speakers assisted to emigrate.

Given nationalists' premise that emigration would cease when Ireland became free, more controversy was inevitable when independent Ireland's rulers generally preferred 'social stability' at home over the adoption of economic policies to stem continued mass migration overseas and, after 1929, principally to Great Britain. Indeed, Ireland's 'possessing classes' regarded those most prone to emigrate as threatening or embarrassing, and, as Lindsey Earner-Byrne describes in the penultimate chapter, this was especially true of pregnant, unmarried Irishwomen who in the 1920s–30s fled harsh communal censure and inadequate social provisions at home for the superior charity and adoption services available in England. In the late 1930s, English protests impelled De Valera's government and the Irish Catholic hierarchy to implement a 'repatriation' scheme for unwed mothers, albeit less from concern for the latter's welfare than from clerical fears that children born and adopted in Britain would become Protestants. Indeed, it was only after 1967, when the U.K. legalised abortion, that either state or church took significant steps to ameliorate the condition of single mothers and their offspring in Ireland.

More in accordance with nationalist ideals was the state-funded, internal migration scheme described by Martin Whelan, William Nolan, and Patrick Duffy in the book's last chapter. Between 1933 and the early 1970s, the Land Commission (building on the work of its predecessor, the Congested Districts Board) sponsored the migration of some 2,600 families from western Ireland and their resettlement on farms in the grasslands of Meath, Kildare, and other eastern counties. Whelan *et al.*, contend the project was generally successful, both for the transplanted farmers and for the eastern districts they revitalised, thus contradicting 'free-market' shibboleths by indicating how beneficial can be the results of benign state planning. However, the *c.* 15,000 people settled in the Irish midlands were but a miniscule percentage of the one million or more Irish who left De Valera's Ireland in the 1930s,

40s, and 50s. And ironically, as Duffy points out in his Introduction to the book, in 1941 it was De Valera himself who, despite nationalist qualms, signed agreements with the British government that legitimised 'a form of systematically-organised emigration that was mutually satisfactory to the economic requirements of both states.'

The individual essays in *To and from Ireland* are interesting and informative. The collection as a whole, however, lacks coherence, because its organising principle, 'planned migration,' is itself insufficient to comprehend successfully all the examples of migration to, from, and within Ireland described in this volume, much less to integrate the instances of conscious 'management' directed by states and/or by economic élites and the private networks of individual and familial 'assistance' that channelled most migrants. Only a more sweeping theoretical framework might have linked all these seemingly disparate movements and processes into a meaningful relationship with global implications. Although Patrick Duffy, in his Introduction, makes a promising effort in that direction, by acknowledging that Irish migration should be viewed in terms of colonial policies and capitalist power relationships, his reiterations of revisionist views concerning 'Irish complicity' in British imperialism, and of neoliberal convictions as to the prevalence of 'individual voluntary [vs. 'planned'] migration,' only obscure ultimate causation and 'flatten' vital distinctions. On another (but related) level, this reviewer would have liked to see a chapter on the official and unofficial migration policies in Northern Ireland to balance the examinations of the Dublin government's performances. Nevertheless, this is a valuable collection, strongly recommended.

KERBY A. MILLER

GERARD MORAN

Sending Out Ireland's Poor:
Assisted Emigration to North America
in the Nineteenth Century

Fours Courts Press, Dublin, 2004
ISBN 1 85182 824 9 pp. 252 €55

It can be argued that, for the first half of the eighteenth century, assisted emigrations accounted for the majority of emigrants' passages across the Atlantic. In the latter half of the eighteenth century, as Louis Cullen has observed in *Europeans on the Move* (1994) 'there was a move from group movement led by ministers, gentry or promoters to a more individual emigration'. The assisted-passage syndrome made a reappearance in a variety of guises in the post 1815 generation of emigration, with the gradual acknowledgement at official level of the need to encourage if not actually take interventionist steps to cope with the grinding poverty of pre-famine Ireland.

Gerard Moran's book describes the range of schemes that were developed post-1815 offering assisted transatlantic fares to tenants on landed estates or paupers who found themselves in workhouses. In this regard, the extent of government participation in assisted emigrant schemes, at least to colonies, principally Canada and Australia, is perhaps the most significant development to arise from the story of assisted passage schemes in the eighteenth and nineteenth centuries. As far as the effectiveness of the government-authorised schemes in helping to reduce the enormous social pressures of an over-populated and famine ridden Ireland is concerned, David Fitzpatrick has pointed out elsewhere that in the thirty years preceding 1845, when one million are estimated to have emigrated, the passages of some 32,000 emigrants were assisted, a ratio of 3.2 per cent. In the subsequent period 1846–52, when manifestly assisted emigration might have been one already-tried means of providing some respite from the ravages of the Great Famine, only 16,000 of those estimated to have emigrated received state-sponsored assistance, a ratio of something like one per cent.

Nonetheless, the numbers are in themselves not-insignificant and, in this context, Gerard Moran's detailed consideration of the schemes that assisted emigrants to leave for North America is both timely and welcome, providing not only a chronicle of the respective schemes in which these 'forgotten emigrants of the nineteenth century' found their way to a new world but painting in the conditions on the estates and in the workhouses from which they were escaping. Moran's consideration of the issue of landlord-assisted emigration from their Irish estates is particularly thorough and confidently handled. On the issue of 'how many?', however, uncertainty persists. Moran's view (p. 36) is that 'While Kerby Miller, Oliver MacDonagh, S.H. Cousens, and David Fitzpatrick vary in their estimates of between 50,000 and 80,000 ... it would appear that these figures are an underestimation. Donald MacKay estimates that the figure is nearer 100,000 and this is perhaps a more accurate reflexion'.

Moran is on stronger ground in his consideration of the motives for landlord-assisted emigration, 'The most important [of which] was to improve the economic condition of their properties'. The political orthodoxy of the day tended if anything to regard the famine as both the means and the opportunity of restoring the Irish economy and society to proportions more manageable than the 8,275,000 population on the eve of the famine could allow. As James S. Donnelly has reminded us, this pragmatic approach 'was the common view of the landed elite'. Nonetheless there is no doubt that, whatever the motivation, landlords' practical intervention enabled at least some instances of distress to seek relief in the more propitious circumstances that most emigrants found on the other side of the Atlantic. In Ulster, the other outstanding example of landlord assistance may be found on the Shirley estate in Co. Monaghan and in this regard Moran has benefited, as have we all, from the published accounts of Prof. Patrick Duffy's research. Duffy has estimated that 'between 1843 and the end of the Famine the [Shirley] estate directly assisted more than 1,500 to emigrate' from this 26,000 acre estate which had over 20,500 tenants by 1845.

The other principal source of assisted emigration was the Boards of Guardians of the 130 workhouses that had been constructed in Ireland in the few years from 1839, almost as a premonition of the outbreak of Famine in 1845. Moran's description of the various degrees of enthusiasm which some, but not all, Guardians greeted the prospect of unloading their over-crowded workhouses is well sourced. It is clear that many of those emigrants being helped to emigrate, either from the workhouses or from the estates on which they lived, were in fact leaving to join members of their immediate or extended family either in the USA or Canada, who would vouch for them on arrival and smooth their entry into a wholly new culture. And this chain-migration process, even though it does not quite comply with the rubric of the title, is adverted to as a fitting postscript, given that it proved to be such a residual characteristic of Irish emigration throughout the nineteenth and twentieth centuries. Moran's conclusion is that 'Even those who arrived in North America with nothing … sent money home to Ireland once they were established. Assisted emigration also played an important role in the chain migration from those areas where it was initiated'. This book, by focusing on those whose emigration was financially assisted by authority, has contributed meaningfully to our wider understanding of the broad canvas that is the story of emigration from Ireland over the last three centuries.

TREVOR PARKHILL

DAVID DOBSON

Ships from Ireland to Early America 1623–1850 Vol. II

Clearfield Press, Baltimore, 2004

ISBN 0 806352 523 pp. 151 $18.50

The issue of how many emigrants did in fact cross the Atlantic from Ireland to Colonial America is one of the longest-running debates in an area – eighteenth century migration – whose understanding at the academic and at the public level has seen very significant developments in the last twenty years. Kerby Miller has, accompanied by David Doyle, Arnold Shrier and Bruce Boling, turned his attention to the emigration characteristics of the 'long' eighteenth century. *Immigrants in the Land of Canaan 1685–1815*, OUP, 2003 (see the review in *Familia* 2003 by David Fitzpatrick) concentrated on the ethnic experiences of the settlers from Ireland north and south and therefore was not in a position to say much new on the numbers that were involved. The fact remains that R.J. Dickson's estimates *in Ulster Emigration to Colonial America* (1966), though generally accepted to be unduly inflated, have not been forensically dissected and reconstructed. Michael Montgomery's article in this volume reports the findings of a recent colloquy of scholars who agreed that 'at least 150,000 natives of Ulster arrived in American colonies prior to the outbreak of the American Revolution in 1776'.

One of the problems has been trying to work out how many people could have gone. This involves an assessment of the population resident in Ireland, the pool from which the emigrants emerged, and also of the number of ships that crossed the Atlantic and the optimum number of passengers they could have accommodated. Added to that, there are no reliable official records of immigrants prior to 1820 (1865 in the case of Canada). Granted that the research of Graeme Kirkham and Marianne Wokeck has tended to direct attention meaningfully away from the numbers game to a more deliberate consideration of the cultural and ethnic characteristics of the transatlantic flow prior to the

1790s, the calculation of the numbers of emigrants from Ulster and Ireland to Colonial America and the United States still represents something of a holy grail.

Ships from Ireland is an alphabetically-arranged list of some 1,500 vessels known to have embarked from ports in Ireland over a period of some 227 years to 1850 and its contents will go some way towards helping researchers compile more informed pictures in relation to both the numbers and the identity of the migrants. Not, it should be said, that it will prove at all possible to trace individuals, given that the information about the passengers travelling does not extend beyond descriptions such as (at best):

> *Brittania*, 500 tons, master John Bryson, arrived in Charleston, South Carolina on 22 August 1767 with 174 passengers from Newry …

or

> *Jessie* a Barque, master William Oliver, from Cork on 5 June with 441 passengers arrived at Grosse Isle on 11 July 1847.

R.J. Dickson, when faced with the issue of how to calculate passengers per ship, used the rule-of-thumb that sailing ships could carry one passenger for every ton. This of course would give only the maximum number of passengers that could have travelled, and also assumes that the weight of the ship has been accurately represented. However, only in a very few cases do the notices of the ships' voyages presented in this volume give both the tonnage and the number of passengers on board. In all of these cases it appears that the 'one passenger per ton' ready-reckoner generally applies. Disappointingly, there are few enough instances of both the tonnage and the number of passengers being provided in the one notice. Where they do exist, they seem largely to substantiate that the 'one passenger for every ton' rule can be applied. 'Belfast Packet of Philadelphia, 100 tons, master Thomas Ashe, arrived in Charleston, South Carolina, with 78 passengers from Belfast October 1766'.

There is also evidence of the true extent of the outflow of migrants from Ulster in the few years from 1771 to the outbreak of the American Revolution, when there was an estimated 10,000 per year from Ulster alone: 'Hannah, master James Mitchell, from Londonderry, with 400 passengers bound for Philadelphia in June 1772; from Londonderry with 520 passengers bound for Philadelphia in June 1773; arrived there 4 August 1773'.

Where the notices are helpful is in the number of times they give details of the inclusion in their passenger complement of indentured servants. David Doyle, in his innovative (though un-indexed!) work, *Ireland, Irishmen and Revolutionary America*, published as long ago as 1981, drew attention to the importance of the indentured servant trade, pointing out that this was long a favoured means of young single men, particularly Catholics, getting themselves across the Atlantic. In doing so, Doyle created some of the parameters for the discussions, still ongoing, about the extent of the proportion of the eighteenth-century migration from Ulster that was in fact Catholic. It had been until then regarded as an exclusively not just Protestant but Presbyterian phenomenon.

One of David Doyle's contentions about the indentured servant trade was that, in addition to it being the means favoured for Catholic emigrants, it continued until well after the date usually associated with its demise, the early 1790s. In this volume there may be some significance in the fact that the two latest dates are each 1784. One of them was the 'Peggy, a brig, arrived in Philadelphia on 28 July 1784 with male and female indentured servants from Londonderry'. In itself this is a rare example of the servants being nominated as being both male and female, an issue that Marianne Wokeck has discussed in a broader European, specifically German, framework in her *Trade in Strangers*.

Wokeck's work has contributed significantly to the ongoing revision of the understanding of emigration from Ireland and immigration into Colonial and revolutionary America. Not only does her research provide a salutary European context for the radical movement of population from Ireland, particularly the Scotch-Irish of the northern half of the island, during these formative decades in the eighteenth and early nineteenth centuries, but her research on the indentured servants' trade and their role in perpetuating the dynamics of the emigration movement has without doubt been among the most meaningful research to have emerged in the last twenty years.

Marianne Wokeck's observations on the theme of indentured servants, some of which have been published in *Familia* (Vol. 18, 2002, pp. 1–20) are amplified by a substantial number of the notices for the eighteenth century in Dobson's book. Those advertising the arrival in America of indentured servants are almost entirely for ships that set out from ports in the southern half of Ireland. For example,

> Sisters, a brig, arrived in Philadelphia from Sligo August 1784 with servants and redemptioners, masons, coopers, tailors weavers, … brickmakers, cabinetmakers, nailers, plasterers and turners.

This would appear to substantiate her observation that, although 'Overall, the total number of immigrants from southern Ireland was small … the proportion of servants among them [was] large, compared with a high total of emigration from northern Ireland, of which only a relatively small percentage were redemptioners and indentured servants'.

The dangers that were an integral part of the emigrant experience are a regular feature of the pages of this book; none more so than the two notices in successive years for 'Faithful Steward, Captain McCausland, from Londonderry bound for Philadelphia in June 1784' with the postscript that it had 'arrived safely in America'. However, the same ship the next year, still captained by 'master Conolly McCausland with 249 passengers bound for Newcastle and Philadelphia in June 1785' was listed as 'wrecked at the mouth of Delaware Bay with 194 passengers drowned'.

There are intriguing reminders of the extent of the other dangers that awaited emigrants who took ship in their bid to get to their New World. Not only were they putting themselves at the mercy of the weather and the effect it would have on the Atlantic Ocean, but they also committed themselves as being hostage to more than fortune, as a number of entries during the 1740s and 1750s indicate:

> Charming Peggy, Captain Ramage from Londonderry to Philadelphia in 1746 captured by the French and taken to Bayonne.

In fact, the French privateers seemed to have something of a (perhaps stereotypically predictable) penchant for any ship called 'Charming'.

> The Charming Molly, Captain Martin, bound from Belfast to Jamaica, captured by the French and taken to Guadeloupe in 1756.
>
> Charming Molly, Captain Redmond, from Cork bound for Halifax in 1761, captured by the French and taken to Martinique.

David Dobson's books have featured regularly in the Reviews section and *Familia* was lucky enough in 2002 to feature one of David's well-researched reminders of the role of Scottish emigration as an important aspect of the Ulster-Scots emigrant experience. Best of all is his capacity to make available for our benefit the results of his meticulous labours, as a he has done here with considerable effect.

TREVOR PARKHILL

D. ROGER DIXON

Marcus Ward and Company of Belfast

Belfast Education & Library Board, Belfast, 2004

ISBN 0 907 102 0 pp. 25 £5.00

The importance of the manufacture of paper in the eighteenth century in Ulster is outlined elsewhere in this volume of *Familia* by Alison Muir. The firm of Marcus Ward and Company dominated the printing business in the city for much of the century, establishing a worldwide renown for the quality of its products and for the innovation of its designs. This catalogue of an exhibition put on in Belfast Central Library by Roger Dixon, Librarian, Ulster Folk & Transport Museum, has the additional advantage of serving as a stand-alone account of one of the most remarkable of the many remarkable businesses in Belfast in the nineteenth century. Many of the designs for which the company became famous were on display in the exhibition and, gloriously in some cases, have been reproduced here in the catalogue in a fitting manner.

In many ways, the most prosaic examples have tended to be regarded, historically speaking, as the most influential. The Vere Foster Copy books, known and perhaps even loved by many hundreds of thousands of pupils who attended Ireland's National Schools, were among the company's financial success, with over 4 million copies being printed. It was in other, more commercial areas, that Marcus Ward found areas in which their expertise in design and colour printing could be seen to best effect. This is readily apparent in the whiskey labels displayed with their colours as rich as when they were first produced. Their other successful specialities, particularly cards and children's book illustrations, are reproduced with equal effect. It is also a pleasure to see represented here what might be regarded as this innovative company's greatest contribution, the production of illuminated addresses – for royal visits, as dedications to respected individuals, etc., – which can themselves now be considered to be an art form.

TREVOR PARKHILL

THOMAS BARTLETT (ED.)

Revolutionary Dublin 1795–1801:
The letters of Francis Higgins to Dublin Castle

Four Courts Press, Dublin, 2004
ISBN 1 85182 754 4 pp. 392 €55.

Thomas Bartlett's contribution to *1798: A Bicentenary Perspective* (the magnum opus of published research on the 1798 Rebellion which he also edited and which was reviewed in last year's *Familia*) considered the effectiveness (or otherwise) of the network of informers throughout Ireland that has traditionally been held to have been among the main contributing factors to the rebellion's failure. Among the most infamous of the informers was Leonard MacNally, himself a United Irishman who was so trusted and regarded with such esteem that it was not until his family, following his death in 1805, claimed the pension that had been awarded him by Dublin Castle that his spying activities became public knowledge.

Francis Higgins, as Bartlett, points, out, did not have the same 'informer' status: 'he never claimed to be anything other than a vigorously pro-Castle newspaper proprietor whose newspaper, the *Freeman's Journal* teemed with invective against the United Irishmen throughout the 1790s'. Originally from a family whose origin was in Downpatrick, Co. Down and which then moved to Dublin, Higgins proved himself to be such a trickster that he acquired the nickname 'the sham squire' that was to stick to him the rest of his life. Arising from his network of informers and his own social contacts, he was able to report to Dublin Castle that (p. 95) 'An invasion still continues the report of the day (more particularly so in the country) as mentioned in my previous letter wherein I took leave to say I would forward you a plan … to keep down the rabble who in every part appear in uniform for plunder …'. The letters are heavily laced not only with information and report of rumours, but with his own opinionated views on political developments and even how they might be handled at government level: (p. 94) 'as long as the R. Catholics through their committees interfere with the lower classes of that persuasion and hold out to them that the Catholics are still oppressed you will find the country disturbed and agitated'.

Higgins was well-placed in Catholic society in Dublin, with the result that he was able to feed 24-carat information through to Edward Cooke, the Under-Secretary who recognised the value of insider information, particularly on United Irish movements in and intentions for Dublin. Control of the city would prove to be crucial come the rebellion and it was one of the network of informers sub-contracted to Higgins, as it were, who led to the arrest of Lord Edward Fitzgerald which fatally damaged the insurgents' plans.

Higgins' letters continued until December 1801 and all 158 of them are here transcribed, edited and indexed by Prof. Bartlett. In addition to these most useful sources, the list of rebels who 'surrendered themselves in the city of Dublin, confessed themselves being engaged in the present rebellion and the number of arms surrendered from 29 June last to 9 September 1798' will prove to be a particularly helpful appendix.

TREVOR PARKHILL

DIARMAID FERRITER

The Transformation of Ireland 1900–2000

Profile Books, London, 2004
ISBN 1 86197 307 1 pp. 704 £30.00

Recent histories, such as Alvin Jackson's *Ireland 1798–1998* (Oxford,1998) and Jonathan Bardon's *History of Ulster* (Belfast, 1994, recently reprinted) have departed from previous 'histories' by bringing the story they seek to tell as close to the present day as can be managed. Earlier in 2004, Roy Foster followed suit in his memorable Wiles History week lectures at The Queen's University of Belfast, 'The Metamorphosis of Modern Ireland 1972–2002'. From a museum perspective, there is the greater expectation amongst the visiting public, particularly those from abroad (and their numbers have been growing significantly in Northern Ireland) that the story of Irish history is brought slap-bang up to date. This of course takes the reader and the author/curator into what is not only a painful past but a past that, being recent, is still vivid in the popular memory.

The issue of whether the historian can include in his narrative events that are still newsworthy is problematic: there may well be a case for adopting (or even restoring) a 'thirty-year rule' to enable the objectivity and the passage of time that is in almost every case required before any historical judgement can be expected to be sure-footed and assured. In terms of the last thirty years, Ferriter's approach is clever (but not too-clever-by-half) and depends to a large extent (indeed this is a feature that generally works well throughout the book) on the published memoirs and writings of contemporary participants or observers, including not only journalists but also sociologists and political scientists. Nonetheless, the last quarter of the twentieth century cannot avoid being seen as something more akin to a chronicle than the in-depth appraisal that characterises Ferriter's consideration of the first seventy-five years.

Ferriter has also been able to call on the sources that have recently become available in the Bureau of Military History files, and includes choice quotations from them with considerable effect, particularly statements from combatants and others involved in the 1913–1921 phase of the revolution in Ireland that created the circumstances for the partition of the island.

Ferriter is very much a new kid who has not been afraid to put his head on the block by telling the story of Ireland in the twentieth century in a holistic context. His punchy confident style, which stops decently short of bravura, the assurance of his writing and research and the boldness of his vision – to narrate the full story up to and including the contents of yesterday's fish-and-chips newspaper wrapping – recommends it for inclusion in the list of books we are frequently asked for in the museum by visitors whose interest in Irish history has been sparked by their visit to the history galleries.

TREVOR PARKHILL

HARRY ALLEN

The Men of the Ards

Ballyhay Books, Donaghadee, 2004
ISBN 1 900935 42 2 pp. 346 £9.99

There is a strong argument for claiming that, in terms of the 1798 rebellion, County Down and County Antrim had their own rebellion, separate from the insurrection that broke out elsewhere in Ireland and particularly in Counties Wicklow and, more seriously, Wexford. There is even a case to be made that the nature of the rebellion in each of the two Ulster counties was significantly different to justify them being treated separately, at least in terms of how they were conducted

Harry Allen does just that in this carefully compiled and richly source-based account of the rebellion in a county, Down, where he has spent all of his professional career. Allen has been one of the leading local history practitioners since the mid-1970s as a researcher and as one involved in the administration of the expanding local historical world. The story of the '98 rebellion in County Down is laced with colourful stories and, if anything, even more colourful characters, some of whom survived the rebellion by one means or another. Allen takes enjoyment in recounting these personal stories as much as he does the account of the two principal military engagements, at Saintfield and at Ballynahinch.

One of the most striking aspects of the bicentenary of the rebellion that was held in 1998 was the extent to which there is still a vividly recollected folk memory in the county. Allen weaves the folklore delicately and sympathetically into the fabric of an admirable use of the wide range of other sources available at local and national level. It would have been nice to have seen an assessment of Thomas Robinson's painting, 'The Battle of Ballynahinch'. Robinson himself was a witness of the battle on 13 June 1798, itself a close-run thing that, had it gone in the rebels' favour, would have made things very sticky, at least in the north, for the government forces. The scene represented on the painting was painted shortly after the battle. Someone with Allen's local knowledge is ideally placed to interpret this primary source, certainly with regard to the individuals clearly sketched on it.

The admirable care and caution that characterises Allen's handling of the evidence, primary, secondary and folklorique, is not mirrored in his writing which manages to convey something of the tension and tumult of the county of Down's role in an episode in Irish history that continues to influence political and cultural identities today.

TREVOR PARKHILL

F.X. McCORRY

Parish Registers:
Historical Treasures in Manuscript

Inglewood Press, Lurgan, 2004
ISBN 095 22161 4 8 pp. 168 £15.00

The parish registers which are discussed in this book comprise Magheralin, Seagoe, Shankill and the Quaker marriage and birth registers of Lurgan as well as the registers of Tynan and Keady. They thus encompass the settlement of population in a large tract of land in north County Armagh with an adjoining parish in County Down, and two adjacent parishes in south west County Armagh. Several of the Church of Ireland parish registers are early ones, commencing in the late seventeenth century – Shankill (1676), Seagoe (1692), Magheralin (1694), Tynan (1684), while the Quaker material covers the period 1655–1707. Additional data on Shankill (Lurgan) and the Montiaghs (Seagoe) carries the discussion down to the end of the nineteenth century and beyond. Thus this book, which is privately produced and printed, brings to a wide readership the fruits of the immense amount of painstaking and original scholarship which has been undertaken by the author during several decades.

Before the various parishes are discussed in detail, an historical introduction outlines the development of parochial registration in Ireland. In 1634 the Anglican Church instructed that records of baptisms, marriages and burials should be kept in every parish in Ireland and so the Church of Ireland registers discussed here can be seen to be some of the earliest in existence. They thus provide insight into life in the post-Plantation period when settlement in Ulster was becoming more stable than previously. Indeed, as Dr McCorry points out, the network and importance of parish structures may have been reinforced by the efforts of these Anglican newcomers in establishing their Church in a way that would be meaningful for everyday living. The introduction also contains a prefatory section , 'A Marriage Prologue', which outlines the historical background to the diverse ecclesiastical and legal interpretations of marriage insofar as these differences affected the marriage ceremony.

This may prove useful to genealogists who have to contend with the practical outcomes of these interpretations.

Taking each parish in turn, McCorry provides an historical commentary which relates to his analysis of the registers. The statistical tables (unfortunately un-numbered) and the commentaries on them reveal an immense amount of demographic data. This is augmented by extracts and information from vestry records. As well as indicating the extent to which vestrymen's activities could be defined as 'early local government' these also include gems touching on the wider world, as in this extract from Tynan Vestry Minutes, 26 December 1709:

> 'that whereas John Corrie furnished ye Guard of Tynan with Candles during ye time that ye pretender was upon ye coast to the value of five shillings and five pence, that ye said sum be assessed in ye said parish, and paid to ye Jn. Corrie.'

This was only two years after the constitutional Union of Scotland with England in 1707. The return from exile in France of James Edward Stuart, the 'Old Pretender', to take up the Jacobite cause of his father James II of England, (also known as James VII of Scotland) who had been defeated for the English throne by William III in 1690, must have invoked immediate alarm in Ulster amongst those who were anxious to preserve new found social stability.

The commentary on Keady parish also includes Derrynoose and this provides information on Roman Catholic and Presbyterian registers as well as Keady Church of Ireland marriage registers in the nineteenth century. Here can be seen two overlapping local outcomes of the food shortages and deprivation of the famine years of 1845–1850 when normal daily routines and seasonal patterns of community activity were, at best, sharply disrupted and, at worst, ceased to function. The disruption can be seen in the Church of Ireland baptism register figures in the 1840s which were one half to two-thirds fewer than in the previous three decades. In the Roman Catholic parish registers of Derrynoose the number of funerals recorded in 1847 was four times higher than in 1850. Fewer baptisms and more funerals speak eloquently of widespread hardship at a local level.

Dr McCorry's earlier scholarly works centre on Seagoe parish,

Lurgan and county Armagh in general and so it is not surprising that a substantial part of this publication is devoted to these districts. As well as the three main denominational registers, the early marriage and birth registers of the Society of Friends in Lurgan and district are discussed against a rich background of information from lease books and other local historical sources, including oral testimony.

This book provides immense minutiae of detail on the selected parish communities. Above all, it draws attention to the worth of the churches' registers as primary source material which record the landmarks of life in a local community. Others who have worked on similar Irish material, such as Morgan and McAfee, Cormac O'Grada and Joel Mokyr and, in England, the Cambridge Group for the Study of Population and Social Structure have long drawn attention to the contribution of such a source in uncovering the interplay between public structures and personal activity. They have also drawn attention to the limitations of such sources whereas McCorry's work almost turns the incompleteness of the denominational registers into a strength. Its most significant contribution may be to encourage others to critically examine afresh other Irish parochial registers, especially those of the pre-Famine period.

BRENDA COLLINS

DAVID M. BUTLER

Quaker Meeting Houses of Ireland

The Historical Committee of Friends in Ireland, Dublin, 2004

ISBN 0 95 19870 6 2 pp. 256 £18/€25

This is a book for the connoisseur in the sense that, fascinating though it is, it can only be dipped into at intervals. Indeed, it is more a gazetteer or book of reference to which one might turn as a point of first reference if researching into Irish Quaker history and the very formative if sometimes underestimated role that Quakers have played in the development of Irish society over the last three hundred years.

David Butler is a Quaker and by profession an architect. Some years ago he published a much larger volume on the Quaker meeting houses of Britain, on which this book is modelled. We are indebted to those who persuaded him to come to Ireland and put on record for the benefit of a wider public the Irish meeting houses. From the perspective of the formal architecture that is associated with what might be called the mainstream churches, it is interesting and, may I say, humbling to read of the sheer simplicity of the Quaker houses and the way of life of those who built them or gave them to the Society of Friends. Butler follows in the Quaker tradition of architecture – there is a well-worn path in Ireland followed by Quaker architects, who are listed in the appendix – and naturally this volume majors on the architecture and design of these houses. They come, to coin a phrase, in all shapes and sizes, from the simplest one-room building to the more elaborate, but still essentially simple and devoid of superfluous decoration, structures found in more (Quaker) populated settlements such as Belfast, Dublin or Lurgan, Co. Armagh. What makes this book doubly valuable is the author's search into Quaker archives in order to unravel the history and, where possible, the design of previous houses used by a particular Meeting. The extent to which the Historical Committee has ensured the preservation of Quaker archives is truly enviable.

Listed alphabetically by province throughout the four provinces of Ireland, Butler has not confined himself to standing buildings or

Meetings that still exist; rather, he has included all those Meetings which either no longer exist or have been amalgamated with nearby Meetings. Burial grounds, both those still in use or long since out of use (and sometimes the exact location of which has been forgotten) are included.

The appendices give us some background to the principles on which meeting houses are designed, the particular form of seating, of heating and other creature comforts and of finance, to mention just a few of the subjects covered.

It is so clearly a labour of love that it might appear churlish to register a reservation or two about a book like this. Although the author has provided copious line drawings (both plans and elevations) throughout the text, this reviewer would like to have seen some photographs of those buildings which still exist, particularly those in larger population centres. The modern eye is more attuned to photographs as they can convey so much more of the context of the building, something a line drawing cannot do. I also feel that a discreet glossary of word usage by Quakers might have been useful to those readers unfamiliar with Quaker phraseology: 'settling' and 'laying down' have a distinctive meaning for Quakers as does the custom of naming the days of the week as First day, Second day and so on. In spite of these caveats, this book is highly recommended and, dare I say it, an essential addition to the library of someone interested in the by-ways of ecclesiastical architecture.

J. FRED RANKIN

Clogher Record
xviii, no. 2 (2004)
Journal of the Clogher Historical Society
ISBN 0 949012 21 1 pp. 205 (Pagination starts at 181 and runs to 386)
Free to members of the society

Local history journals are an important though frequently overlooked source of information of interest to genealogists. For over fifty years the *Clogher Record*, the journal of the Clogher Historical Society, has maintained a consistently high standard in its output. This year's issue does not fail to disappoint with eight articles and a number of shorter notices. Several of the articles are of particular interest to family history researchers. Theo McMahon's article on the Rose estate at Tydavnet in County Monaghan is based on documents rescued from being discarded from a house in the town of Monaghan. As well as discussing the background and development of the estate, Mr McMahon includes a list of the tenants arranged by townland from rentals of 1840–1. A useful map of the estate is also provided.

The focus of June Brown's article is also on a landed estate in County Monaghan: the Dartrey estate owned by the Dawson family. Drawing on documents in the Public Record Office of Northern Ireland and other sources, Ms Brown looks at the fate and fortunes of the Dawson family as well as the creation, development and disintegration of this estate from the seventeenth century to the twentieth. This article includes a number of colour photographs and line drawings, including an elevation of the family home, Dawsongrove, from *c.* 1770.

Donald Schlegel presents an index to the insurgents, identified alongside place-names, recorded for County Fermanagh in the depositions of 1641. This is a particularly valuable tool of reference for as the compiler himself has pointed out 'the documents serve the useful purpose of identifying some of the Irish inhabitants who otherwise would be unknown to us because of the lack of any other records' (p. 319). In the Notes and Comments section there is an interesting account of the discovery of two previously unknown gravestones in Donagh graveyard, County Monaghan – a reminder that, frequently, research in old burial grounds is an ongoing process. All in all, another excellent production and worthwhile reading for anyone interested in the area covered by Clogher diocese.

WILLIAM ROULSTON

Familia: *Ulster Genealogical Review* no.19 (2003)

Ulster Historical Foundation, Belfast, 2003
ISBN 1 903688 40 X pp. 144 £5.95

A RETROSPECTIVE REVIEW

You hold in your hand the twentieth instalment of a most worthy enterprise. As the index in its immediate predecessor shows (see Vol, 19, 2003), a very considerable range of material has steadily been gathered in this *Ulster Genealogical Review*. The first volume (1985) set a consistent standard, balancing articles of wider historical and (auto)biographical import with all-important practical advice on the challenge of researching more or less elusive Irish ancestors. Arguably, all local history has genealogical implications even, at a bureaucratic pinch, when a former Stormont mandarin writes in Number 17 about his peers and indeed himself. An earnest, perhaps, of an autobiography in progress?

Perusing Number 19 in the immediate aftermath of the XV Ulster-American Heritage Symposium (held at the Ulster-American Folk Park, Omagh, June 2004), one sees anew how *Familia* has particular value for students of the very precise business of migration. Christine McIvor traces in common-sense categories the evolution of the Atlantic voyage in the nineteenth century. Appropriately, the volume's cover reproduces J.H. Connop's lithograph (1853) of her home city on the Foyle, Londonderry having been a major port of departure for the vast parish which was North America. Richard K. MacMaster writes specifically about the voyage of the *Nancy* from Belfast to Charleston South Carolina in 1787.

Given the undisputed importance of the emigrants' letters, the student who had recently been ranging far and wide in Kerby Miller *et al.*, *Irish Immigrants in the Land of Canaan* read with more than usual interest David Fitzpatrick's strenuous structural review. Was Miller indeed 'jaded' by his literary and historical endeavours, 'heroic' or not?

Privileged with a cache of family documents, some 1,000 letters discovered in Molenan House, Londonderry, Richard Moore-Colyer excavates the story of his 'ain folk' on both sides of the Atlantic from the eighteenth century onwards. Regarding Ulster Presbyterian emigration to America, Elodie Aviotte opens up a classic comparative issue – the absence of a Unionist political dimension in North America – which is all the more relevant in changing political times in Northern Ireland.

The index already mentioned does not provide details of the many publications noted and reviewed in *Familia* over the years of almost two decades. But the tradition of the permanent log is well maintained under the editorship of Trevor Parkhill to whom, if memory serves, goes the aboriginal credit for suggesting the compact, genealogically most apt title for this annual. His predecessor until 1993 was Kenneth Darwin, whose very sharp pen was in evidence as recently as Number 18. Of a new generation of reviewers, Jonathan Hamill amplifies well the many interpretative possibilities in newspapers in nineteenth-century Ballymoney and Coleraine. The present writer, who spent a splendid evening simply turning page after page of the Coleraine volume (1844–1869), knows well that knowledge of the townlands can maximise the genealogical implications of a 'wee' word here and a local link there. Similar thoughts are provoked by James O'Hanlon's article on newspaper reports of violent deaths in Ulster.

Other reviews deal with publications on the European linen industry, re-evaluations of 1798 Rebellion, the townlands of Portavo, and the Office of Arms. William Roulston's attention to the genealogical relevance of this last complements Duncan Scarlett's item on the Registry of Deeds. In 2003 *Familia* again offered fine fare.

EULL DUNLOP